TON

Jeffrey Brantley, MD
Wendy Millstine, NC

five good minutes in your body

100 mindful practices to help you accept yourself & feel at home in your body

New Harbinger Publications, Inc.

Publisher's Note

This publication is designed to provide accurate and authoritative information in regard to the subject matter covered. It is sold with the understanding that the publisher is not engaged in rendering psychological, financial, legal, or other professional services. If expert assistance or counseling is needed, the services of a competent professional should be sought.

Distributed in Canada by Raincoast Books

Copyright © 2009 by Jeffrey Brantley and Wendy Millstine
New Harbinger Publications, Inc.
5674 Shattuck Avenue
Oakland, CA 94609
www.newharbinger.com

Cover design by Amy Shoup; text design by Amy Shoup and Michele Waters-Kermes; acquired by Tesilya Hanauer; edited by Kayla Sussell

All Rights Reserved. Printed in the United States of America.

Fifth in the Five Good Minutes™ series

Five Good Minutes is a trademark of New Harbinger Publications, Inc.

Library of Congress Cataloging-in-Publication Data

Brantley, Jeffrey.
 Five good minutes in your body : 100 mindful practices to help you accept yourself and feel at home in your body / Jeffrey Brantley, and Wendy Millstine.
    p. cm.
Includes bibliographical references.
ISBN-13: 978-1-57224-596-9 (pbk. : alk. paper)
ISBN-10: 1-57224-596-4 (pbk. : alk. paper)
1. Mind and body. 2. Body, Human. I. Millstine, Wendy, 1966- II. Title.
BF151.B73 2009
158.1'2--dc22

                                    2008039791

10   09   08

10   9   8   7   6   5   4   3   2   1   First printing

This book is dedicated to anyone who ever struggled or suffered in their body. May you rediscover your wholeness and live with ease and happiness.

—Jeffrey Brantley

For Mother Earth, from whose infinite wisdom and bountiful body all life issues forth. May I always be humble and grateful for her many gifts and remain worthy of her sacred guidance.

—Wendy Millstine

contents

mindful movement   93

feeding your body's senses   145

introduction

Do you live *in* your body or *with* your body?

Both, of course (and more).

Imagine living more happily and completely in and with your body—not only your physical body—but inside your wholeness as a human being.

What if your relationships with yourself, with others, and with the world could deepen and become enriched as you learned and practiced inhabiting your own body with greater awareness and more compassion?

Finding greater happiness and fulfillment in your life might begin with this interesting question: *What is your current relationship with your body?*

Are you more often in touch or out of touch with it?

Are your thoughts about your body dominated by judgments and criticisms? Or by interest and curiosity?

Are your attitudes toward your body driven by fear or dislike? Or by gratitude and compassion?

It's easy to become confused about your body. In these times, and especially in this culture, practically everyone is bombarded by complicated and often conflicting messages about what it means to be an embodied and whole human being.

Visual images of idealized bodies that are alternately seductive, repulsive, exciting, frightening, and even shocking surround us.

Advertising messages, often in the guise of promoting health and well-being, leave the (intentional) impression that whatever your physical (or emotional, psychological, even spiritual) condition might be—it is not good enough—and requires something else (most likely the advertiser's product)!

And many, if not most, people have very little accurate and current information regarding recent scientific discoveries about the amazing connections between the mind and body, and the implications of these connections for improved health and happiness.

One profound and disturbing consequence of all these conflicting messages is that you are often left feeling both fragmented and compartmentalized regarding your basic experience of being human, moment to moment and day to day.

Yet your path to greater health and a happier embodiment—to being more consciously present in your body moment by moment—could be closer and more accessible than you ever imagined.

Finding that path depends, in part, on the recognition that humans are whole beings inhabiting bodies that change, which are built of collections of smaller bodies (atoms, molecules, cells, tissues, organs, and so on) and which simultaneously belong to collections of larger bodies (pairs, families, groups, species, ultimately, all living things). Your mind and body are deeply interconnected with each other (indeed not even as separate as those terms imply), and with the flow of experience through the larger (and smaller) bodies around (and within) you.

So finding your path to better health and a happier embodiment depends on being present. Experiencing wholeness grows from cultivating your awareness of the amazing interplay between your body's sensations and functions and the flow of your thoughts, emotions, and attention, literally breath by breath.

Mindfulness

What if all it takes for you to find greater happiness and better health in every aspect of your life, as you go about your daily routines in your own body, depends simply on paying attention on purpose, in a kind and nonjudgmental way, right now in the present moment?

Mindfulness is the name for the awareness that arises from paying attention on purpose, in a gentle and welcoming way, moment by moment. Mindfulness is a basic human capacity that can be strengthened with practice. *Being mindful* simply means paying attention on purpose, nonjudgmentally, with an accepting, friendly spirit.

Mindfulness can be applied to your body, to the smaller "bodies" it includes, and to the larger "bodies" it belongs to.

And, very importantly, mindfulness (which includes the qualities of kindness and compassion) can be applied to your body when it is ill or in pain, as well as when it is healthy and vigorous.

In the practices in this book, you are invited to discover how gentle nonjudging attention centered in the present moment and focused on your body, in all of its expressions, can set the stage for a radically different—and more rewarding—experience of embodiment, and of life itself.

Presence, Intention, Wholeheartedness

In our previous books in the *Five Good Minutes* series, we offered easy, accessible, mindfulness-based practices that can be done in just five minutes of "clock time," and yet they hold the power to profoundly transform your life.

The power in these practices is that they invite you to step back from unconscious and automatic habits of mind and body dominated by rush, worry, and the momentum of busyness, inattention, and distractions.

By coming off of autopilot and intentionally returning to the present moment with your full attention, you return to the only place where life is actually happening—here, in the present moment, where you have the opportunity to experience yourself, others, and life itself more fully and authentically.

The five-good-minutes method is simple and consists of three elements: *presence* (which is based in mindfulness), *intention,* and *wholeheartedness.*

You come into the present moment more consciously by being mindful, setting a clear intention, and from the base of presence and intention doing a specific activity, or practice, wholeheartedly.

These are both the keys to your "five good minutes," and the vehicle for transforming five minutes of simple clock time into five minutes of being vibrantly alive, radically new, and filled with possibility.

In our earlier books, we applied the principles of mindfulness, intention setting, and wholehearted action—in the form of easy five-minute practices—to subjects ranging from daily life to evening hours to work situations, and to love relationships.

This book invites you to apply the power of being present, setting an intention, and acting wholeheartedly toward the experience of being in your body; and even more explicitly, to exploring consciously and deeply what being embodied can actually mean to your moment-by-moment experience of being alive and in relationship with others. If being present, setting intention, and acting wholeheartedly sound like confusing or overly simplistic concepts, don't worry! You'll be given very clear instructions, and you can move at your own pace to explore the practices.

Kindly and Consciously Inhabiting Your Own Body

Your body is always with you, at least for as long as you are in this life. Yet the moment-by-moment relationship you have with your body can be a source of either great pleasure and comfort or of pain and upset.

The five-good-minutes approach offers anyone—busy or not, well or ill, young or old, female or male, at ease or in pain—a powerful opportunity for self-discovery and transformation.

By learning to inhabit your body more consciously and in a kinder way, you will build a base for a wiser and healthier relationship with your physical body and with your inner life. And you'll very likely find a more authentic and satisfying presence in the world for yourself.

The organizing themes for this book are "Inhabiting Your Body," which is about being more conscious of your sensory experience of your body; "Mindful Movement," which focuses on your experience as a moving body; "Feeding Your Body's Senses," which deals with nourishment in its many forms; and finally, "Wise Body," which is about accepting and loving your body.

The final theme points to the importance of kind feelings and compassion when relating to your body, in all its various states and conditions.

Inhabiting the Body of the World

In each of these sections you will find new and interesting ways to be in your body and to explore your place in the larger body of the world. You will be encouraged to have fun, be curious, make discoveries, and be surprised!

You will be invited to reflect upon and to sense the life in and around your body more deeply, never forgetting that the earth brings us into the light and takes us back again, and that the elements of water, fire, and air constantly support and inform us about the mystery and sacred blessings of this human life.

So, however you choose to work with *Five Good Minutes in Your Body*, the 100 practices you will find here can help you rediscover and reclaim your own body. The practices will also help you to engage with the body of the world in authentic, playful, and wise ways. As you actually experience these practices, you'll find they offer you the possibility of:

- connecting with and moving more consciously in your body—and in your life

- accepting and nurturing your own health and happiness and that of others

- finding a safer and more welcoming home in your body—and in the world

Welcome to *Five Good Minutes in Your Body!*

PART 1

the foundation

At Home in the Long Body of Your Life

Five minutes is just a concept. Two "hands" move over a numbered surface, and from your eyes' interaction with that activity, your mind forms the thought *five minutes*, and an entire cascade of events may follow in your mind and your body.

Your mind and body are deeply interconnected with each other and with the flow of experience through the larger and smaller bodies in and around you. Amazing interactions and interpenetrations between physical and energetic forms are constantly occurring, providing you with the foundation for all of your life.

When you bring your kind, nonjudging attention to this foundation, and to the flow of all experience there, you may come (in your own time) to a realization of the sacred mysteries embedded in the long body of your life. And you will find yourself truly home in your body and in the world.

The beauty and complexity of life take place only in the present moment.

And the present moment is always here and is always timeless. Your life unfolds in the present moment and your body is always here, too, alive and changing in the moment, as life flows through and around it.

As physical experience flows through your body and this moment, so do your thoughts and feelings. Even your thoughts about the past or future also take place in the present moment.

Because of the amazing connections and feedback loops between mind and body, the very thoughts you have about your body can either limit or expand your experience of life in this moment, as well as the degree to which you can *experience* your body and feel at ease and be at home and comfortable in it.

The 100 practices in this book are intended to help you discover new dimensions to being embodied; they aim to promote a greater appreciation of the possibilities for happiness and healing inherent in our bodies. And they are meant to support you in finding a true home in your body and in the present moment, even if you have never felt at home in your body or in the world.

Along the way, you may find yourself developing a wiser and more nurturing relationship with your body, a relationship characterized by:

- caring more and obsessing less
- nurturing without abusing
- holding what is dear more closely than ever
- letting go, ultimately, of everything, peacefully

Why Five Good Minutes in Your Body?

Are you ever driven more by thoughts about your body than by the actual experience of it?

Are your thoughts filled with fear or meanness, or some other distortion?

16

Are you sometimes so busy that you live apart from your body, either slightly ahead of or behind it, lost in your thoughts about your past or future?

Have you ever felt like a prisoner inside your body, unhappy and disconnected, wanting only escape?

Unfortunately, in today's world, almost everyone can answer yes to one or more of those questions. Young or old, sick or well, short or tall, thick or thin, any color, any shape—almost everyone, at some time, has been simultaneously preoccupied with and out of touch with their own body.

The 100 practices offer you the possibility of creating a wiser and more compassionate experience of and relationship with your body. Doing the practices can become a path of self-discovery toward a more authentic embodiment in your life; literally making yourself both more real and more fully alive.

The practices can be done in just five minutes of clock time, but their power comes from you making yourself available for a radically different experience of living in your body. You do that by being mindful and present with clear intention as you wholeheartedly engage the suggestions in this book.

How to Use This Book

The 100 practices are organized and grouped according to four main themes. The first theme, "Inhabiting Your Body," encourages you to use mindfulness, intention, and wholehearted activity to be more present for the direct experience of your body; for example, to really notice the physical sensations and experience of hearing, without being hijacked by judgments or story making.

The second theme, "Mindful Movement," invites closer attention to the diverse experiences associated with movement in and by your body. These practices take a fresh look at your familiar habitual movements throughout daily life; they also include movements done mindfully for their own sake.

"Feeding Your Body's Senses," the third section, focuses on the many sources of nourishment available to you. You will find five-minute-practice opportunities to work with the foods you eat and the liquids you drink and with your other sources of nourishment, such as rest, silence, and joy.

The final section, "Wise Body," emphasizes the heartful qualities of affection and compassion. It invites you to explore ways to practice these qualities and bring them forward more explicitly to enrich your relationship to embodied living.

Doing the practices in each of these sections will help you to realize more deeply your wholeness as an intelligent human being, blessed with greatness of heart and an amazing body.

It will also help you to let go of any old stories you may have about your body, and to create a new experience of caring for it—just as it is. This will free you from negative thoughts that no longer serve you. It will open you to more self-love and acceptance, which will allow you to be a more powerful force in the world.

You will find practices for healthy bodies as well as for sick bodies or bodies in pain. In addition, there are practices for bodies of any age.

In each section, you will find some practices that invite you to use the foundation of your own bodily experience to remind you of your connections to larger and smaller bodies, and of the interconnections and interdependencies of all living things. These will help to inspire and affirm you in finding your true place in the body of the world.

When doing your practices, please keep in mind the following:

- You do *not* have to do all 100 practices to benefit.

- You do *not* have to like or enjoy all 100 practices to benefit.

- You definitely do *not* have to work through the practices in any particular order or sequence to benefit.

- Despite the title of the book, you are definitely *not* limited to five minutes for your practice or to only one session each day.

What is most important is to *do* your chosen practice—not just read about it. It is only in the doing that you will experience the full potential available in each practice. And, when doing your practice, it is truly useful to approach it in the spirit of relaxing and having fun. Remember, you cannot make a mistake or do anything wrong. No one is watching or grading you. So let go of the idea of "fixing" anything, and allow yourself to be buoyed by the spirit of curiosity and experimentation. Letting go of attachment to specific outcomes will add immensely to your discoveries and enjoyment of these practices.

It is also good to be patient with yourself. Take your time. Read through the practices in any order you choose. Some people like to simply open the book and work with whatever comes up. Others develop a strategy for their practices; for example, doing the same one daily for a week or doing one from each section daily, or any other way.

Look for practices that appeal to something within you. When one sounds like fun, awakens curiosity, or evokes an actual feeling of relief or ease in your body, that would be a good place to begin.

You will probably find that it helps to read through the practice a few times before actually doing it. At times, you may want to ask someone to read it to you. Or you may wish to share the practice with another person or even a group. Practicing together can be very rewarding and can even deepen relationships.

Finally, over time, you will probably discover that you change daily, as does your work with the practices. What appeals one day can change, and what happens each time can actually be fresh and unique.

For that reason, it can be very valuable to go back from time to time to review the sections, opening yourself to different and untried practices, as well as to the familiar ones. You will find that approaching each practice with "beginner's mind"—as if you had never seen it before—will support a spirit of exploration, curiosity, and discovery that will carry you a long way.

Mindfulness: Your First "Good" Minute

You are living in your body now, in the present moment. Life happens only in the present moment. Yet it is so easy to be distracted, pulled outside of yourself, and to lose sight of what is most important. Establishing a receptive attention in the present moment is the first minute of your five good minutes.

Anything you do after coming into presence through mindful attention becomes richer and more alive. In fact, you may feel richer and more alive. Practicing mindfulness is your doorway to the present moment.

You already have what you need to be mindful. Mindfulness is a basic human capacity for present-moment awareness. Mindfulness is *not* thinking. It actually recognizes when thoughts are occurring, just as it notices sights, sounds, and sensations as they are happening.

Mindfulness arises when you pay attention on purpose in a nonjudging, friendly, and allowing way to experience life flowing by in the present moment.

Being present, being mindful, also includes trusting and learning to rest in your inner feelings of stillness and spaciousness, and experiencing a greater sense of peace and ease, moment by moment.

Throughout this book, you will see instructions like "Breathe mindfully for about a minute," or "Mindfully tune in to the sensations flowing in your body."

These instructions simply ask you to access your natural ability for presence and awareness by directing your attention in a particular and intentional way. Doing this is easier than you think.

You will find easy-to-follow instructions below for mindful breathing and for mindfully tuning in to the sensations flowing in your body.

Return to these instructions for practicing mindfulness as often as you like. Make them your friends, and learn to trust yourself to become more mindful in every moment of your life.

Practicing Mindfulness

Although you already have a natural capacity for mindfulness, it helps to develop that capacity as a kind of skill, through practice.

You practice mindfulness simply by deciding to pay attention nonjudgmentally and affectionately more often and in different settings, and then doing it.

With mindfulness, you do not practice to become perfect; instead you learn what it means to be mindful (or not mindful), and to trust yourself that you truly can be mindful, no matter how great the challenges you face. And, as you practice mindfulness more and more, you will likely find that it will spill over, arising and benefiting you in other moments and situations where added presence and awareness are valuable and welcome elements.

Doing any of the 100 practices in this book mindfully will help you to strengthen your natural capacity for mindfulness. Many of these practices provide explicit encouragement or different methods for practicing mindfulness.

Although you can be mindful of any experience, there are two methods for practicing mindfulness that repeatedly appear in this book: They are to focus either on the sensations of breathing or on the sensations in your body. Because these methods appear so often, more specific instructions can be found below.

Instructions for Breathing Mindfully

① You can practice breathing mindfully in any posture, in a still body or a moving one.

② If you can do it safely, you may wish to close your eyes to reduce distractions.

③ Begin by remembering that during this meditation you do *not* have to make anything happen, or become anyone other than who you already are. You can trust that you already have all you need to be mindful.

④ Now, gently focus your attention at the place in your body where it is easiest for you to feel the sensations of your breath as it comes in and goes out of your body. It could be at the tip of your nose, your mouth, your chest or abdomen, or somewhere else. Let your attention rest there.

⑤ Allow the focus of your attention to be on the direct sensations of breathing. You do not have to control your breath in any way. If your mind creates a picture or image of the breath, let that go. Gently and patiently return your attention to the physical sensations of the in-breath and the out-breath and the stillness, or pause, between them. This is an awareness exercise, *not* a breathing exercise nor a visualization.

⑥ As your attention steadies and becomes more sensitive, begin to notice the changing and varied sensations. Notice, for example, the rising and falling of your abdomen or chest, the coolness or warmth of the breath, and its smoothness or roughness. Relax and let the breath come to you. Practice allowing and accepting each sensation just as it is. Let each breath sensation carry and support you more and more steadily and deeply into the present moment.

⑦ When your mind wanders or something distracts you away from the breath sensations, you have *not* done anything wrong. You have *not* made a mistake. It is simply how the mind moves. Acknowledge this movement and patiently return your attention to the breath, letting the next breath in. There is no need to hurry or fight thoughts, sounds, or other distractions. No need to follow them either.

⑧ Continue practicing this way: letting the breath support you; having kindness and patience with the movements of your mind and other events; and being attentive and present for just this breath, the one that is happening now.

⑨ End your meditation by shifting your focus from the breath sensations, opening your eyes, and moving gently, if you like.

Instructions for Mindfulness of Bodily Sensations

① You can practice mindfulness of bodily sensations in any posture, moving or still.

② If you can do it safely and it helps you focus, let your eyes gently close.

③ As in all mindfulness practices, for the time of this meditation, remember that you do not have to make anything happen or become anyone other than who you already are. Trust that you already have everything you need for mindfulness.

④ Gently bring your attention to the experience of feeling your body sensations. Collect attention in the places it is easiest to feel them, perhaps your arms or legs, the pressure and contact of your back against the chair, or the sensation of air on your bare skin.

⑤ Relax and let the sensations come to you.

⑥ As your attention steadies and your awareness becomes more sensitive, open to the variety of sensations flowing throughout your body. Notice heaviness, pressure, vibration, dryness or dampness, contractions and releases, for example. You may like to practice placing your focus on particular parts or regions of your body and noticing the sensations there. Or you can practice moving your attention systematically from one part of your body to another until you have connected with your whole body.

⑦ When thoughts or stories about your body, or other distractions, arise, you don't have to fight them, and you don't have to follow or feed them. Just let them go and return attention to the direct sensations, allowing them to come to you just as they are. When your mind wanders, no matter how often, you have *not* done anything wrong. Have patience and kindness for yourself.

⑧ As your attention become steadier, allow it to be light and soft. Notice any tendency to hold on to one sensation or to get rid of another. Let go of any urges to cling to or to reject any sensation, and return your focus to the direct experience.

⑨ When you are ready to end your practice, release your focus from the sensations, open your eyes, and move gently, if you choose to do that.

Intention: The Second Element of Your Five Good Minutes

Setting a clear intention is a way of pointing yourself in the direction of an important value or goal. In fact, intention precedes all goal-directed movements in our human bodies, so it's good to learn to identify intention and to practice setting wise intentions.

The 100 practices in *Five Good Minutes in Your Body* all involve setting and acting on intention. Many of them invite you to be very explicit and actually put your intention into words. You can use the examples provided for specific intentions or you can create your own.

Know that you can be skillful or unskillful when setting an intention.

For example, it would not be very skillful to set the intention to never have pain in your body or to never feel upset, and to expect that you can actually achieve that as a goal.

When setting your intention, be careful not to pick an unrealistic one or put pressure on yourself to achieve it. That would be an example of an unskillful intention, one that is actually a setup for harsh judgments, self-criticism, and possibly despair about your ability to do anything successfully.

The skillful intention is much more effective.

A skillful intention is more like a friendly guide. It reminds you of your destination and points you in the right direction, while acknowledging that important changes, as on any journey, take time. Patience, kindness, and compassion for yourself are invaluable allies for your skillful intention.

So although an intention to never feel pain in your body isn't realistic, a reasonable direction would be to feel more at home in your body and more adept at handling any pain you do feel.

A skillful intention does not demand instant or dramatic results. It does not give up when impatience and frustration appear. Instead, when challenges and doubts arise, the skillful intention simply becomes more resolved, kinder, and more patient.

Acting Wholeheartedly: The Final Piece of Your Five Good Minutes

Acting wholeheartedly means doing something with all of your attention and available energy. It means making your best effort. If you have already established mindfulness and set your intention, you will have built a sturdy foundation for wholehearted action.

Again, it is always wise to be skillful and understanding with yourself.

You may find it takes some practice to be wholehearted, even for five minutes. Much of what we do is done without full attention or commitment for a variety of reasons. The habits of inattention and disconnection can be overcome, but at times it may take some effort, some patience, and some willingness to laugh at your foibles.

Acting wholeheartedly also goes more smoothly if you can act without attachment to the outcome. In other words, just do it!

For example, if you are doing a practice that is intended to foster peace and relaxation in your body, then don't get stuck by constantly checking to see "is it working yet?" Instead, relax and just do it, mindfully noticing whatever happens.

Wherever your chosen practice takes you is fine. Just do it, mindfully, with intention, and as wholeheartedly as you can, and you will very likely learn something useful. Or you may discover something within you that needs care and attention. Or you may have a deeply rich experience or simply have some fun.

There is a paradox operating in the 100 practices in this book (and very likely in other parts of your life, as well). The paradox is that although you do want to change and for things to be different, the more you demand change, pushing and pulling or fussing and fighting, the slower the changes will come, and the more likely you are to become frustrated and discouraged.

So when doing your practice, see if you can let go of the attachment to a specific outcome, no matter how appealing the result may seem. Instead, just pay attention and you might discover something you had not planned for or thought you needed—or believed could happen. Try giving life a chance to surprise and amaze you or even teach you something new. Each time you practice acting wholeheartedly, you give yourself another opportunity to be surprised and awakened by life. And that surprise and amazement can occur in other places in your life!

Finally, it is perfectly okay if you find yourself feeling silly, embarrassed, or awkward, or anything else that seems out of character, as you act wholeheartedly doing your practice. Those feelings are probably just a reflection of some inner story or judgment you are still holding on to. Remember, you cannot make a mistake as long as you give it your best effort. Doing your Five Good Minutes is *not* a performance or a competition!

So, let curiosity, kindness, compassion, patience, and humor accompany you as you explore different practices, and give yourself room to grow and learn.

A Gift to Yourself and to the Body of the World

The 100 practices in this book—using mindfulness, intention, and wholeheartedness—invite you to become more at home in your own body, and to find your true place to stand with greater authenticity in the body of the world. Doing even one of the practices can be a profound and sincere gift you can offer to yourself.

Learning to connect more deeply, to move more consciously, to nurture, and to have more mercy and affection for your own body will naturally help you bring these qualities forward in other places and relationships in your life. Countless others may benefit as well.

It is our deep and sincere hope that you will find happiness and healing in these practices, that your body, mind, and spirit will be amazed and awakened, and that your own unique and precious life will continue to flower, bringing greater peace and joy to yourself and to the body of the world.

PART 2

the practices

inhabiting your body

1

reinhabit your body

Reconnecting with and inhabiting your body more consciously can happen simply by paying attention more closely and more often—without judgments and with affection—to the physical sensations flowing throughout your body.

Take a few minutes as often as you like to consciously reinhabit your body using this practice. Enjoy yourself and delight in self-discovery.

① To begin, set aside other activities and distractions.

② Let a spirit of curiosity and appreciation arise in you.

③ Set your intention. For example, "May this practice teach me about my whole being."

④ Gently bring your attention to the changing sensations flowing through your body. Notice them directly: the solidity of your bottom on the chair, the pressure of an elbow on the table, the vibration of your heart beating, the warm air as it flows out through your nose, the coolness of a gentle breeze on your skin, and so on.

⑤ Try to narrowly focus on a specific part of your body, such as your forearm or right cheek. Then move to another part of your body, and then another.

⑥ When thoughts arise, notice them, and let them go without struggling with them.

⑦ Return to the sensations in your body. Feel the life flowing inside you.

2

body talk

Have you ever noticed how many of your waking hours you spend in your head, rattling off chores to add to your to-do list, mulling over past emotions, or just generating endless thoughts? Where is your body in all this thinking? What's your body doing and feeling while you're ignoring it? Let's find out.

① Take this quiet moment to really pay attention to your physical body.

② What is your body doing right now? Are you slouching, at ease, or tense?

③ If your body had a voice, what would it say to you? Would it remind you of your lower back pain? Would it ask you to do a few stretches to unwind and relax? Maybe it is asking you to sit upright and uncross your legs. Maybe your eyes are tired after staring at a computer screen all day and they need a break.

Take this time to listen to your body. When you hear what your body is saying, you will reconnect with it in deeply healing ways.

3

rewrite your pain story

The longer your body holds pain—from illness or injury—the bigger the story your mind creates about that pain. Over time, a single thought about the pain can evoke anxiety or fear, adding tension to your body and increasing your suffering.

To disconnect from pain's story and promote total healing, try this practice.

① Noticing your pain or discomfort, breathe mindfully for about a minute.

② Set your intention. For example, "May this practice support my healing."

③ Mindfully pay attention to the body part in distress. Softly open as much as you can to feeling the sensations there. Imagine breathing mindfully into and through the area as you observe and allow each sensation.

④ When thoughts arise, notice them and let them go, not fighting or following them.

⑤ Return to the sensations and your breath. Let the peace you feel comfort you.

4

body alignment

How does work affect your body? If your job requires physical labor, you may be putting severe demands on it. If your work involves sitting for long periods of time, your body endures different stresses. Let's dedicate the next five minutes to aligning yourself with your body, and promote wellness from within.

① Take a break from work and begin by focusing on the rhythms of your breath. Observe whether you're taking short, shallow breaths, or breathing more deeply from your chest or belly.

② Acknowledge how your whole body and any areas you may be neglecting feel. Take note of any pockets of tension, tightness, soreness, or fatigue. Where does discomfort live in your body—your head, neck, shoulders, back, or feet?

③ Say aloud or to yourself, "With each out-breath, I am releasing pent-up tension and stress. With each in-breath, I am restoring physical well-being." Repeat these words throughout your day to realign yourself with your body's health and healing.

5

seeing mindfully

Wen you look at something, what do you see?

Have you ever truly observed the color, shape, or texture of a flower? Or is your mind so busy creating its idea of a flower that you don't see the real flower in front of you?

Watching a sunset, do you see the shifting patterns of light and form as they change, or does your mind tell you a story that holds you?

Connecting with your body begins with each of your senses—if you are mindful. To explore the wonders of mindful seeing, try this practice.

① Pick any object or scene to practice seeing mindfully.

② Set your intention. For example, "May I learn to see more clearly."

③ Breathe mindfully for a few breaths.

④ Consciously shift your attention to seeing a particular object or a part of an object, such as liquid in a glass, or sunlight on a leaf. Notice the experience without focusing on thoughts; instead focus directly on colors, shapes, light, shadow, motion, and space around the object.

⑤ When thoughts do arise, gently let them go without struggling or following them.

⑥ Return patiently to your direct visual experience.

What did you discover?

6

media break

In our media-saturated world, it's easy to be impressed by flashy photos of glamorous models with sexy, thin bodies airbrushed to perfection. But have you noticed how you feel about yourself after you've been inundated with such unrealistic images of beauty? When was the last time you thought about how the media reinforce the myth that only skinny people deserve love? You don't have to buy into this false message. Be mindful of the creative ways that can free you from the influence of these unhealthy images, which can sabotage your happiness.

- Toss out or stay away from glossy fashion magazines and pick up a good book.

- Shut off the TV, or at least mute the commercials, and pick out a movie that touches your heart, lifts your spirit, or reconnects you with humanity.

- Go for a walk, get outside, tend to your garden, or go to the gym.

- Call a friend, make a date, cook a meal together, and exchange stories.

- Give yourself a break. Soak in a bath and take solace in the silence.

7

sounding good

Humans can make an amazing variety of sounds. Your voice can be a flexible tool to convey and display who you are and what you feel. Notice that: each sound does not require its own, separate thought. A sound, by itself, can be a powerful and revealing reflection of your life.

To explore and enjoy "sounding," try this mindful practice.

① Choose a place where you feel free to express yourself with sound, and you won't disturb others.

② Take any comfortable position, making sure your body is well supported.

③ Breathe mindfully for about a minute.

④ Set your intention. For example, "May I have fun and discover something new."

⑤ Bring your attention to your throat and chest.

⑥ Slowly and softly release any sound or tone waiting there; give it energy and attention using only your voice.

⑦ Breathe and repeat your sound, perhaps with more energy. Do it again. Try making higher and lower tones.

⑧ Enjoy sounding good!

8

find your warm spot

Ever notice how dogs and cats enjoy nestling in the warmest spot in the house? It's usually where sunlight breaks through a window and warms up a rug or a bedspread. The pet can relax and sleep for hours on end. If you could have a warm, safe, and cozy space to rest your weary body, where would it be?

① In a seated position or lying down, close your eyes and imagine the most comfortable place in your home. Maybe it's your bed or couch, underneath a cherished blanket, a comfy chair with soft pillows, or your partner's embrace.

② Take note of all the pleasurable details of your spot. What's special and inviting about it? Make a mental list of those qualities, such as quiet, snuggly, warm, and protective.

③ What emotions do you experience in this safe place? Make a mental list, such as peaceful, at ease, safe, and content.

④ Carry this memory of your restful spot with you and remember that it lives inside you wherever you go.

9

walking barefoot

So many of life's wonders are always present in this moment, waiting simply for your attention.

Walking mindfully can be a fun and often amazing reminder of the joy of embodiment.

For an unexpected sensual treat, try doing your mindful walking barefoot.

① Pick a place to walk where you won't be interrupted. The more textures and surfaces there are, the better your bare-foot walk will be. If outdoors, walk on earth, grass, or sand. Indoors, try walking on carpet, wood, or tile.

② Get barefoot, and breathe mindfully for about a minute.

③ Set your intention. For example, "May this practice reconnect me, with joy and wonder."

④ Let your attention settle mindfully on your bare feet. Notice the direct sensations there—pressure, vibrations, coolness, and warmth.

⑤ Slowly begin walking. Stay focused on the flow of direct and changing sensations. When thoughts come, smile and release them. Return your attention to the sensations in your feet and enjoy each one.

⑥ Let joy and surprise fill and nourish you as you walk.

10

body betrayal

A dear friend of Wendy's sometimes has sciatica—a form of excruciating lower back pain that is utterly debilitating. She cannot move or find any relief for days on end. She once said that it felt like "her body was betraying her." If you live with physical pain, especially chronic pain, then it's likely you are all too aware of the ways in which your life revolves around your pain. The next practice guides you on how to bring mindful healing into your sore spots.

①   Identify and focus on the places in your body that store pain, inflammation, or tenderness—shoulder strain, stomachache, tennis elbow, knee pain—wherever it hurts.

②   Place your palms together as if praying, and rub them briskly and vigorously for a few seconds until you create a warm tingling sensation in your hands.

③   Once your hands are warmed up, place them carefully and gently on the body part that hurts or aches.

④   Say aloud or to yourself, "In this moment, I am listening to my body speak. I am giving kind attention to my shoulder (or knee or whatever) to help my body focus and to restore healing energy."

Move gently and safely throughout your day.

11

the joy of the world

The energy flowing between you, your body, and your connections with the body of the world can be consciously appreciated—if you pay close enough attention.

Let this practice of mindful listening to a larger body tune you in to the joy of the world.

①   The next time you are part of an audience or group of people who are laughing, decide to explore the energetic connections of joy.

②   Set your intention. For example, "May this practice inspire and enliven me."

③   Direct your mindful attention to the sounds of laughter; notice the loudness, the high and low tones, the rising and fading sounds, and the quiet spaces.

④   As thoughts or stories arise in your mind, let them go without following them.

⑤   Notice the sensations in your body as the laughter flows around you. Enjoy the moment as your body feels the joyful energy flowing through it.

⑥   Take comfort in the sounds of joy. You are part of this laughter and human connection.

12

I feel it in here

Many people are cut off from what their bodies are feeling, unaware of how their emotions manifest physically. Whether you're aware of it or not, emotions often can be first detected in the body. Do you know that different people experience the same emotion differently? When you feel rage, you might feel a tightening in your head—like a headband being pulled too tight—or a burning in your gut. Another person might feel rage and literally see red, as if he or she were wearing red-tinted glasses. How do emotions express themselves in your body?

①   What emotions are you feeling right now? Are you under pressure, frustrated, impatient, or resentful? Do you feel exhausted, depleted, and ready to snap?

②   Once you've identified what you're feeling, pay attention to what is happening in your body. Are you hot or cold in certain places? Do you notice any tension or pain in one area?

③   Focus on the specific regions of your body where your feelings are manifesting, and imagine breathing into them. On your in-breath, visualize comfort and understanding. On your out-breath, visualize release and relief.

④   By paying attention to the subtle emotional movements in your body, you reconnect with yourself in profoundly healing ways.

13

be where you are

Your body is now here.

But your attention may be in three places: the past, present, or future.

One enlightening alternative to the habits of disconnection and inattention is to pay attention to your body's total sensory experience mindfully, in this very moment.

In other words, keep your mind where your body is, and be where you are.

① In any situation you choose, decide to explore a deeper connection, and to open to any greater happiness that may be available.

② Set your intention. For example, "May I be at peace and filled with joy."

③ Breathe mindfully for a few breaths.

④ Widen your focus and mindfully include the flow of all bodily sensations in your awareness.

⑤ Relax, and gently allow your breath and bodily sensations to come to you.

⑥ Widen your focus again and include other sense experiences: sounds, smells, and tastes.

⑦ Notice any thoughts that arise, as well, then release them without struggle.

⑧ Inhabit this moment, experience life deeply, and be where you are.

14

a mirror of compassion

Some days, your own inner critic may harass you for being too fat, too bald, or too old. Don't allow this harsh opponent to hijack your self-esteem. To cultivate compassion for yourself, practice this next mindful visualization.

Seated comfortably, eyes closed, take a few slow, deep breaths, and feel your body loosen and relax. Imagine you are sitting in a chair in an empty white room. The room is peaceful and quiet. There is a revolving door at one end of the room where positive and negative thoughts enter and leave. As critical thoughts of your body come into your mind, imagine them as feathers circulating around the room before being whisked out again.

Observe your thoughts and let them flutter effortlessly in a circle around the room. You can see the thoughts fly in through the door, and then whisk out again. Notice how thoughts come and go.

15

no mind reading allowed

Do you worry about how other people perceive you? Do you consider yourself an excellent mind reader who knows what others think about you? Maybe you've thought, "He's disgusted by my weight" or "She can tell I feel bad about being short." The truth is no one can read others' minds, and it's probable that when you try, you guess wrong. So let's take a moment to meditate on quieting the mind reader.

① Think back to the last time you made up a story that someone was judging you negatively. Did you draw your conclusions from facial expressions, body language, or tone of voice?

② Ask yourself if it's possible that you misinterpreted a dismissive tone or gesture, not realizing that the person may have been feeling equally insecure, self-conscious, or intimidated.

③ Consider how you came to have this special mind-reading power, and ask yourself if it serves you anymore. Imagine erasing your inner mind reader and surrendering to the reality that you may never know what another is thinking.

16

you are precious

Many people struggle with low self-esteem that interferes with their ability to hold on to a positive image of their body. You may think, "I'm too short" or "I have ugly skin" or "I'm flabby and not athletic." Such negative thoughts deplete your sense of self-worth. This next meditation will enhance your sense of self-worth.

Take a few relaxed breaths and quiet your mind by letting go of any critical thoughts about yourself. You are not the sum total of these destructive thoughts. Your self-worth cannot be measured or based on the negative stories you tell about yourself. We know this because all human beings have some goodness, or value, that cannot be taken away or measured.

In this meditation, remind yourself that your value doesn't depend on your body size, or birthmark, or pimple. We are all born flawed. Perfection does not exist. You are a rare and cherished gift of creation. We were never meant to compare ourselves with others. You are worthy, worthwhile, and precious.

17

anger is not you

You are not your anger.

Anger is an intense, volatile, commanding energy that moves through you.

Sometimes anger may feel as if it has taken control and is consuming you.

To take back control from anger, try this next practice. Apply mindfulness to your whole bodily experience of anger.

① The next time you are angry, use mindfulness to manage the feeling.

② Set your intention. For example, "May this practice free me from anger's control."

③ Breathe mindfully for a few breaths.

④ Open your focus, and mindfully notice the physical sensations flowing in your body, including the feelings of anger.

⑤ Note where your anger feels strongest and how it feels. Does it burn, freeze, grip, or pound? Breathe mindfully with your angry feelings, allowing them room and watching them change.

⑥ Notice any thoughts that accompany or feed the physical feelings of anger. Smile at the thoughts. Let them go. Don't fight or follow them.

⑦ Have mercy on any pain you discover beneath your anger.

18

recharge your body

You may push yourself like a battery-powered perpetual-motion machine. No breaks. No naps. No downtime. You may be so run-down that fatigue and exhaustion are running your show. You know your body is worn down, but you still drive yourself to do the next task. Take a time-out for a few minutes of meditation to rest and recuperate.

Relax into your body and reconnect with your natural breathing rhythm. Let your body slump in your chair. Let your arms and legs go limp. Take this time to visualize recharging your internal battery by magnetically drawing in positive energy.

Feelings of hope, love, openness, and serenity drift across the room and deposit themselves into your body. You begin to feel a sensation of warmth and calmness spreading slowly over your entire body. In a short time, you will return to your busy schedule feeling refreshed, refocused, and recharged.

19

sacred you

Many people experience their bodies in predominantly physical ways. When you think of your body, you may think of what you like or dislike physically, such as your face, skin, body size, or agility. Can you imagine a relationship with your body beyond the limits of your physical characteristics? One that goes deeper than how you look? Try this meditation to awaken a more soulful relationship with your body.

At the center of your being lives your soul. Visualize your soul as a radiant, golden beam of light near your heart or in your belly. This inner light represents all your beauty, strength, resiliency, and other positive qualities. It is your spiritual core. It isn't troubled by physical shortcomings or limitations. Focus on this light that represents your soul and breathe into it—imagine the light growing in intensity and radiance with each breath in and out. Nothing and no one can touch or take away your sacred light, which connects you to your body.

20

breathe mindfully

Your life is happening now, in the present moment, and you already have everything you need to inhabit your life—and this moment—completely.

For these five good minutes, let the practice of mindful breathing bring you home again, to your wholeness in this present moment.

① Take a comfortable position in a place where you won't be interrupted.

② Set your intention. For example, "May this practice revitalize me."

③ Gently bring your attention to the sensations of your body breathing. Allow and welcome all sensations without preference or judgment.

④ For the rest of this session, practice mindful breathing. Remember this is a practice of awareness and presence, not a breathing exercise.

⑤ Meet any thoughts that come to you with kindness and mercy, not fighting them, but noticing, allowing, and then releasing them.

⑥ Keep it simple. Breathing, noticing, softening, opening, and returning to the breath sensations with patience whenever your attention wanders.

21

stand tall

When faced with confrontation, your body may want to become smaller, as you shrink from dealing with the troubling issue. You might hide or distract yourself from facing a possible quarrel. You might feel scared and inadequate. But when you shrink from expressing your feelings aloud, you minimize how important good communication is to you and the other person, whether it's your partner, friend, parent, or child. The next meditation will help you to feel grounded, right-sized, and capable of coping with the challenge of communicating your needs.

① The next time a confrontation cuts you down to size, observe your posture. Are you slouching, drooping, or feeling discomfort in any parts of your body?

② Breathe into the parts where you feel tension, and feel yourself more firmly and consciously rooted in your body.

③ Notice how you might adjust your body to sit or stand taller and more upright, with your shoulders back and head held high. As you elongate your spine, you are becoming more right-sized, equal to others, with the courage to stand up to challenges, and to speak the truth from your heart.

22

be patient

Practicing mindfulness, you quickly notice your attention wanders and your mind "has a mind of its own." Be patient with yourself. Keep it simple. Remember to practice patience the way you practice mindfulness of bodily and sensory experience—in the present moment—the here and now. Over time, observe how your "patience" practice touches the other parts of your life.

① Wherever you are, decide to inhabit this moment mindfully and patiently.

② Breathe mindfully for a few breaths.

③ Set your intention. For example, "May I become more present, awake, and open."

④ Widen your focus to notice your total experience in this moment: Notice sensations, sounds, tastes, smells, thoughts, and feelings.

⑤ When your attention wanders, practice patience with yourself and refocus on the sharpest experience happening now.

⑥ When you notice upset feelings or irritation, practice being patient with them. Act as a parent soothes an upset child; hold your upset with kindness, mercy, and patience. And refocus mindfully on that experience.

⑦ Keep it simple. Practice mindful attention supported by patience, trusting yourself, softening into this moment, embracing wholeness, and your life.

23

disrupt your jealousy

It happens to everyone. You're standing in line at your favorite café when you spot a good-looking, effortlessly fit couple, and you immediately hate them. You don't know them. You can't imagine their personal story or struggles. Yet you are filled with utter jealousy. You may even think, "How dare they parade around here when I'm feeling supersensitive about my body." Let's take five to disarm your feelings of inadequacy.

① Find a place to sit and be still with your feelings. You may find a table at the café or return to your car. Notice where in your body you feel this feeling of jealousy. Is it in your chest? Your stomach?

② Consider for a moment that you have before you two distinct paths you can follow: One direction leads to anger, hatred, and separateness. The other points to empathy, compassion, and unity. Take a minute to imagine which path will bring the greatest overall benefit. Which is more likely to reward you with peace of mind and body?

③ Now imagine taking small baby steps away from your jealousy or envy. Say aloud or to yourself, "When I walk the path of envy, I only hurt myself and others. When I walk the path of acceptance, I generate more warmheartedness for myself and others."

This meditation gives you an opportunity to be mindful of how jealousy erupts in your body and gets in your way by keeping you from experiencing kindness and nonjudgment toward others.

24

make room for grief

Sorrow and grief are inevitable companions on our journey through this life. And grief seems to have a mind of its own—moving through mind, body, and spirit in its own time and own way.

Health and happiness can be directly affected by how skillfully you work with and relate to the feelings of grief and vulnerability moving through this moment of your life.

Let this practice help you connect more consciously with the grief in your body, and let it pass.

① When you become aware of grief, or sadness related to loss, arising in you, stop and take a comfortable position where you feel safe.

② Breathe mindfully for about a minute.

③ Set your intention. For example, "May this practice promote healing."

④ Breathe mindfully for a few more breaths.

⑤ Gently widen your focus and include the physical sensations of grief you sense, wherever they live in your body. Notice heaviness, contractions, pulsing, and clenching. Include any sensations of crying as well.

⑥ Relax, breathe mindfully, and continue to soften and open around your sadness. Hold it with affection and mercy, and hold yourself the same way. Drop resistance to this moment— let it all be; let it all go.

⑦ Breathing, compassionate, present, and allowing, what do you notice?

25

awake in your moving body

Could there be a wise still place within you that recognizes, welcomes, and allows the river of changing sensations that is your moving body?

What if becoming more awake in your body were as simple as learning to focus steady, nonjudging, and affectionate attention on the sensations in your body as you move naturally through daily life?

To see what you can discover about stillness and motion, try this practice.

① The next time you are on the move, in a hurry or not, decide to move mindfully.

② Set your intention. For example, "May this practice awaken wonder and amazement in me."

③ Focus mindfully on the strongest sensations you feel as you move. Notice the direct sensations—pressure, vibration, contraction, and expansion—allow them, and let them go. Keep moving naturally.

④ Let your attention become increasingly steady and sensitive. Open to subtler and briefer sensations—a pull here, a touch there, temperature, moisture.

⑤ Notice and release any thoughts, without clinging to or struggling with them.

⑥ Awake and present in your moving body, rest in appreciation and wonder.

mindful movement

26

body rapture

The great Sufi poet Rumi believed that just to be embodied and alive to our senses is cause for ecstasy and rapture.

How does your body move during times of joy and happiness?

① Make a mental or written list of a few events in your life that filled you with delight and bliss.

② In those special memories, what was your body doing? Were you lying down with a lover? Were you dancing your heart out to your favorite music? Were you giggling madly with an old friend, reminiscing for hours on end?

③ What sensations did you experience during those fun times? Did you feel your heart expand? Were you out of breath but overflowing with energy? Did your belly tingle?

④ Now that you've observed what joy feels like in your body, you need only tap into your joyful memories to remind your body how to turn on the bliss.

27

walk mindfully

Would you like to:

- Escape from the grasp of hurried and worried thinking?

- Recover your attention from the past and the future?

- Enjoy the wonder of being alive here and now?

These and other benefits could be easier to achieve than you think—if you learn to practice mindful walking.

Mindful walking simply means placing nonjudging and friendly attention on the flow of sensations arising, changing, and fading as you walk. And there is *no* speed limit. (Although it is often easier to start slowly.)

① Pick a path for walking, or decide to pay mindful attention when walking from one place to another.

② Set your intention. For example, "May this practice awaken me."

③ Bring kind and open attention to the flowing sensations arising as you walk. No need to imagine or force anything. Relax and notice the sensations of contact, motion, contraction, extension, vibration, and so on. Notice the quality of the air and light around you, the sounds that you hear, and the smells. Let them come to you at their own speed.

④ Let go of any thoughts that come, without fighting or following them.

⑤ Relax and enjoy! You cannot make a mistake.

28

head, shoulders, knees, and toes

Do you occasionally notice that you have cold hands and feet? Maybe you work in an office with poor heating or a drafty window. This exercise will help you improve your circulation and keep you warm.

① Begin by taking a deep breath and blowing into your cupped hands. Then, vigorously rub your hands together until you create a warm friction.

② As you rub, imagine the warmth that you're creating with your hands flowing to your torso, legs, arms, and down to your feet.

③ From a sitting or standing position, reach for the sky with your arms and hands. Next, drop your hands to rest on your head, then your shoulders, belly, hips, thighs, calves, and feet. Then start over and repeat this exercise three to five times, gradually increasing the speed of your movements.

Notice how this brisk movement not only warms you up, but also helps your body relax.

29

move mindfully and safely

Whether working at a desk, being physically active, doing chores at home, or traveling for your daily commute or even farther, you move a lot in one day.

Cultivate the habit of paying mindful attention while you are moving. It can help to protect you from accidents—and the cumulative injury of repetitive stress syndrome—caused by inattention or impatience. You may also find yourself enjoying the trip more along the way.

① During any activity you choose, decide to practice mindful movement.

② Set your intention. For example, "May being mindful protect and energize me."

③ Without expecting any specific outcome, gently begin to notice the position, movement, and sensations in your body during the activity. Make slight adjustments if, in your mindfulness, you notice your body is out of alignment or wants to reposition itself.

④ Sharpen and strengthen your focus by placing it on the strongest sensations that your movements evoke.

⑤ When thoughts arise, just smile and release them without struggle.

⑥ Let patience support you as your attention returns to the sensations again and again.

⑦ May mindfulness protect and energize you.

30

listen and learn

Your body is a teacher that already knows the way. There is great wisdom stored in your body—but you've got to slow down, focus, and listen attentively to comprehend what it's telling you. The next exercise gives you an opportunity to take a gentle five-minute walk. As you head out the door, imagine that you are a student walking in the footsteps of a wise teacher. You are the student. Your body is the teacher. Your teacher has seen the road ahead and will guide you safely.

① On your walk, pay attention to your gait. Are you walking fast, slow, or erratically?

② Tune in to your posture. Take a moment to make comfortable adjustments to feel more aligned and upright.

③ Notice how your body instinctively knows just what to do and where to go, what to avoid, and how to maneuver safely around it.

④ Who's leading whom? Is your body deciding the path or do you always walk in this direction? Perhaps your body chose a new direction and you're following.

⑤ Your body knows where it wants you to go. Allow it to guide you.

go with the flow

In a crowd of bodies, you literally become a part of the body of the world. Moving in that crowd, what do you feel? Where is your attention?

Next time you are in a crowd, try the following practice—and let mindfulness awaken your sense of connection and ease your passage through the world.

① Finding yourself in a moving crowd, decide to practice flowing mindfully.

② Set your intention. For example, "May I move freely and with ease."

③ While moving, begin breathing mindfully for a few breaths.

④ Widen your focus, and include the sensations of your moving body in your mindful awareness.

⑤ Notice and gently release any thoughts that may arise.

⑥ Whatever your speed, refocus on the sensations of your body moving.

⑦ Widen your focus to include the energy of the crowd. Notice how the crowd flows with the energy—quick, steady, stalled, swirling—and how the energy flows through the crowd. Let yourself feel the energy flowing in your own body.

⑧ Relax and go with the flow.

32

busy fingers

Today, most people are well up to speed with computers, cell phones, iPods, and technological gadgets that keep their fingers busy all day long. If you use these tools, you may experience soreness or discomfort in your finger joints at night. The following exercise is to bring more awareness to your overworked underappreciated hands.

① Start by shaking out your arms, hands, and fingers at your sides. Allow everything to loosen up and wiggle freely.

② Now take a good look at your gloriously perfect hands, and say hello. Maybe you haven't noticed how hard they work for you, what you put them through, and what you expect of them daily.

③ Take this moment to thank all of your fingers for the many things they do for you, such as opening drawers, locking doors, typing, writing, cooking, chopping, and answering the phone.

④ Be kind to your hands, appreciate them, give them a break from time to time, and don't forget that a little pampering goes a long way.

33

act locally

Would you like to bring more peace and ease to the world?

You can, perhaps more quickly than you realize.

Finding yourself in a moving, agitated crowd—in an airport security line, for example—note that your own "vibration," expressed by and through your body, can either add to the chaos or create a peaceful space. Try acting locally to promote peace by using the following practice.

① When you notice a larger body's agitation, decide to do something to help.

② Breathe mindfully for a few breaths, then expand your focus. Include the flowing sensations in your body as part of expanding your focus.

③ Notice and release any angry or upset thoughts you may be having. Don't fight them and don't follow them.

④ Gently and patiently return attention to your breath and body sensations as you continue moving with the crowd.

⑤ Let the peace of moving mindfully fill you and radiate into the space around you.

⑥ Give thanks for the gift of peace.

hug me!

Everyone loves to be touched, hugged, and held. Like everyone else you need affection. Who wants to live without it? Physical intimacy through touch is a vital part of your happiness. But what if you just don't get enough, or you live or work alone? Take the next five minutes to love yourself and don't be shy.

① Sitting or standing, put those arms of yours to work and reach across your chest and hug your body.

② Give it a long, good squeeze.

③ Think about the thousands of embraces that you've received in your lifetime, and the thousands that you've given to others to comfort, celebrate, welcome, and say good-bye.

④ Say aloud or to yourself, "With this hug, I am sealing in all the love, all the kindness, and all the reassurance that I need."

35

kick and grin

Picture a baby on her back in the crib—wiggling her arms and legs and smiling.

Or imagine a dog happily rolling in the grass, kicking his legs in the air.

Such joyous pleasure lives in your body, too. It waits for your attention.

Totally for fun, try the following practice.

① Make sure your back is well supported, and then lie down on the floor (use a yoga mat if you have one), or lie on the ground if you are outdoors.

② Close your eyes, relax, and breathe mindfully for about a minute.

③ Set your intention. For example, "May I have some fun!"

④ Slowly start to move, and bring mindful attention to your body sensations.

⑤ Maintaining support for your back and body, allow your body to move as much as it likes, at any speed. Kick, roll, stretch, flex, and shake, just like a baby or a dog.

⑥ Notice your widening grin, and let it fill you.

⑦ Wahoo!

36

workout awareness

Everyone has a different preference for exercise. It could be yoga, swimming, biking, or running. Exercise is an excellent way to build strength, muscle tone, and burn calories. It's also a way of connecting wholeheartedly with your body and deepening your relationship through movement. There are numerous ways to infuse your exercises with more mindfulness. Let's try some now.

① While you're engaged in your physical activity, focus on your breath. Make sure you are not holding your breath. Pay attention to whether you're breathing through your mouth or your nose.

② What's happening with your heart rate? Is it fast or slow? Be aware of where you feel your pulse beating the most rapidly— head, neck, wrist, heart, or elsewhere.

③ Throughout your workout, notice your body and skin temperature. Did you just begin your workout and you aren't warmed up yet? Or are you hot and sweaty from a really good workout?

④ Keep up the good workout! Your body loves you for it.

at your edge

Much can be learned about ourselves and the unconscious reactions of our minds and bodies simply by paying attention mindfully, while we hold a body position or pose.

Yoga teachers often invite their students to "explore their edge" in this way.

The exploration can be any position. Play with the following gentle practice for increased self-awareness.

1. Take any safe and well-supported position you like.

2. Breathe mindfully for about a minute.

3. Set your intention. For example, "May this practice bring me flexibility and wisdom."

4. Mindfully inhale as you move one or both of your arms out to your side, forming a right angle with your torso. Keep breathing mindfully as you hold your position. Holding.... Holding....Breathing....Holding.

5. Let your mindful attention include and allow all the sensations arising in your body, without struggle. Notice any thoughts and release them without struggle. Keep breathing mindfully, letting it all be as it is.

6. Exhale mindfully, and let your arms float down to a resting position. Notice how that feels.

7. What have you discovered about your body and mind?

38

listen up!

We are a visually dependent society. Your entire life is arranged and dictated by sight—what you can see—often to the neglect of other vital sensory perceptions. Let's zero in on your magnificent ability to hear. By bringing your hearing into your more immediate consciousness, you'll become more mindful of this miraculous gift every day.

① Cup your hands over your ears, as if to prevent sound from entering. What sound still comes through? Is it muffled or quiet?

② Uncover your ears and hang your hands by your sides.

③ Now close your eyes, let your mind rest from your endless thoughts, and focus only on what you can hear in your immediate environment. Do you hear the clock ticking, the refrigerator humming, the heater blowing? Did your belly just growl? Did you hear your neck pop or crack?

④ What do you notice about the sounds outside? Maybe a car passed by, or a bird sang, or perhaps you can hear your neighbor's stereo.

⑤ Listen and pay attention. For just five minutes allow yourself to experience life through your ears.

39

tickle your funny bone

Laughter is truly the best medicine. Science confirms that laughing releases endorphins—the hormones that encourage us to feel joyful and blissed-out. When was the last time you had a good fit of giggles? Take this moment to delve more deeply into your funny bone's memory.

① Where were you during your last laughing jag? Who were you with? Maybe you were watching a movie, playing with your children, or roughhousing with your dog.

② What kind of laughter was it? Were you chuckling or snorting? Was it belly laughter? Or were you doubling over in hysterical giggles?

③ What sensations do you experience in your body when you laugh so hard that it nearly brings you to tears? Perhaps your body starts to shake and tremble all over, heat up, and then perspire. Does your face get flushed and warm?

④ Ever noticed what your mouth is doing? What about your hands? Do you try to cover your face at such raucous times?

⑤ Let your amusement run wild while you surrender to the memory of this hilarious free fall of laughter.

40

bowing to the world

The act of bowing—intentionally stopping, gesturing respectfully, and bending lower—can be a powerful tool for a more conscious relationship with yourself and with others.

Let this practice of bowing to the world awaken and reveal inspiring and generous dimensions within you, and within all of your relationships.

Over time, by extending this practice into more and more moments of your life, you may find that you are appreciating each moment in an increasingly sensitive and deeply moving way.

① Breathe mindfully for about a minute.

② Set your intention. For example, "May this practice open my heart to more gratitude and respect."

③ Bring mindful attention to your entire body. Feel the flow of sensations that represents the flow of life within you.

④ Bring your hands together in the prayer position.

⑤ Recall someone or something that was beautiful and inspirational to you, and gently bow. That person or inspiration might also be here with you now.

⑥ As you bow, if you like, add words like "thank you" or "may you be well."

⑦ Finish your bow. What have you noticed?

41

empty the stress storeroom

The body does a great job of stockpiling stress. Then it might break out in muscle tension and stiffness. It could also manifest as a pounding headache, burning indigestion, or a racing heart. You can ignore stored stress for a short while, but eventually it creeps back in and demands your attention. Let's take this next five minutes to explore tender and nurturing ways to relieve body stress.

① When your stress levels are maxed out, how does that affect your body? Maybe your immune system collapses and you catch head colds more easily. Perhaps stress hits you during a meal and you get terrible heartburn.

② Because it's nearly impossible to avoid stress, what are some creative ways you might use to tend to discomforting flare-ups? Take a short break and go for a walk. Run some refreshing cool water over your hands and face. Make some herbal tea and drink it while checking in with a coworker or friend.

③ Take a quiet moment to check in with your body. Don't be afraid to ask it what it needs to feel nurtured and cared for.

42

appreciate the little movements

Countless overlooked little movements of daily life hold the potential for encouraging gratitude and awakening presence to the mystery and miracle of being alive.

This practice invites you to bring mindfulness to such movements and moments. Keep it simple. Without requiring anything other than your close attention, gently begin noticing what is happening with your body more often, as it carries you through the day.

① Pause during any ordinary physical activity to become more mindful of your bodily sensations and changing movements—moment by moment. For example, notice the movements of your feet and legs after you get out of bed to stand up and start walking. Observe the actions of your thumbs and fingers while dressing. Notice how the muscles flex in your arm and hand when you're chopping vegetables.

② If it helps you to focus, breathe mindfully for a few breaths. Softening and opening, notice your bodily experience with increasing sensitivity.

③ Keep it simple. Don't get lost in thoughts or plans. Bring attention back to your body and your five senses. Open to touch, motion, stretching, and holding. Notice the amazing variety of movements your body accomplishes in the routine activities of daily life.

④ Hurrah! Give thanks. You are alive, embodied, and awake.

43

park it in the moment

A great deal of our life is spent sitting. You might work at a desk eight hours a day. Then you sit for meals, watch TV, drive the car, or commute by subway. When you are bored, tired, or discouraged about life, you might sit down.

Is it possible to be more mindful while you're parked in a seat? Try this next meditation for instilling awareness even while you are just sitting.

① From a seated position, take a couple of slow, deep breaths, feeling the air glide in through your nostrils and then move out again.

② Observe how your body feels right now. Are your shoulders tight? Are your eyes weary? What about your lower back?

③ Notice how sitting takes the weight off your feet. What are your legs and feet doing? Are they crossed over to the right or left? Are they resting on a rug or a wooden floor?

④ How you can make yourself more comfortable? Do you need to stand up, stretch your arms, or take a sip of water? Make those adjustments now and notice how these changes make your body feel.

44

permission to stop

Momentum is a powerful force.

Once you are in motion, the tendency is to keep moving. And your movements, especially when hurrying and worrying, can be in both body and mind. All you need to stop the momentum of mind and body begins with giving yourself permission to stop.

Try this practice and see for yourself.

① The next time you are feeling rushed, acknowledge that feeling with compassion for yourself.

② Set your intention. For example, "May I find more self-compassion and ease through this practice."

③ Physically stop moving.

④ Breathe mindfully for a few breaths.

⑤ Open your focus and notice any remaining sensations of movement in your body. This is your momentum, still present. Notice too the sensations in the parts of your body that are truly still and not moving.

⑥ Recognize any worried or hurried thoughts with acceptance. Let them go. Don't fight or follow them.

⑦ Ask your body and mind, "Is it okay to stop now?"

⑧ Listen to your body. How does stopping feel?

45

put your body to sleep

You spend almost one-third of your life sleeping. Restful sleep is crucial for the body to repair and heal itself. Without it, you feel overtired, overwhelmed, achy, and irritable.

Just before you go to bed, take a few moments to check in with your body.

From a reclining position on your back, feel your body surrender to this restful moment. Notice your breathing—the slow, rhythmic, rise and fall of your chest and belly. Your arms and legs are relaxed and becoming heavy. You can feel your back and buttocks sink further into the mattress. You may notice that your eyelids are getting heavier and heavier. The weight of your head is descending further into the pillow. Any areas that might have been holding tension are now releasing and falling, letting go, and drifting off. From head to toe, your body is completely relaxed and still.

46

dancing with anger

Anger is an intense and disturbing energy that occupies and moves through the body.

Too often, for many reasons, people struggle to bottle up their anger.

Have you ever considered moving with your anger instead of trying to contain it, as a way to manage it more skillfully?

Try working with anger mindfully by using your body and some humor.

① When you notice feelings of irritation, frustration, or just plain anger, decide to work mindfully and compassionately with the upset.

② Set your intention. For example, "May this practice empower me."

③ Breathe mindfully for a few breaths.

④ Now open your awareness mindfully to all the sensations moving in your body.

⑤ Notice the sensations and energy of anger. As you begin feeling anger's energy in your body, allow that energy to move you. Let your body lead you, stretching, shaking, punching, or kicking.

⑥ Allow your movements to become a dance. Let your body dance, harmlessly releasing anger's force and energy.

⑦ Gently conclude the dance. What is happening now?

slowing down

As you age, you may begin to notice that you can't run quite as fast you used to or move as swiftly; or maybe you lack agility, dexterity, and flexibility. This is not a time to wallow in regret but rather an opportunity to give yourself permission to slow down—there's no reason to hurry. Here's a mindful reminder to take your time and be gentle with your body.

① Instead of lamenting your lost youth, take this moment to fully accept your body as it is today.

② Say aloud or to yourself, "Today my body is telling me that there are some things that I can still do with ease and grace. I can walk, work, make love, and take care of most things in my life. I am grateful for these gifts."

③ When you slow down and move at a more leisurely pace, you reduce the possibility of injury and mistakes. You begin to accept—and love—your body exactly as it is in this moment.

48

morning surprise

Once that blaring alarm goes off in the morning, most folks ease their way out of bed and head for the shower, giving little thought to what's going on with their body. Let's do it differently this morning and start with a mild stretch for your lower back.

① Begin by lying on your back, eyes closed.

② With your arms resting at your sides, wiggle your toes and feet, hands, and fingers.

③ Now lift your legs, bending and hugging your knees to your chest. If you can, hold this position a few minutes.

④ Feel the stretch in your lower back. Notice how your abdominal muscles are relaxed at this time.

⑤ Now release your grasp of your knees and allow your legs to recline and relax. Pay attention to any tension or tightness in your body. Then do this stretch again.

You're now ready to begin your day with greater ease and flexibility.

what if? as if

Your body moving through the world is just one part of larger moving bodies.

You are one person in a crowd; one car in a traffic jam; one member of your family or your work group.

What if you could release—even a little—the tensions of "I, me, mine," and sense and befriend some other members of the larger body?

Act as if you can. Act as if your attention, steadiness, and compassion—in this moment—for all the others, really does benefit all of them.

① Pause and notice the larger body flowing around you in any moment.

② Breathe mindfully for a few breaths.

③ Set your intention to explore a larger dimension.

④ Mindfully notice—looking, listening, sensing—the larger body all around you. Breathing mindfully, soften into the fullness of this moment, allowing it to be.

⑤ Offer good wishes to all. "May everyone here be at ease."

⑥ Move ahead with kindness and clarity.

50

pockets of joy

Even the most menial and tediously boring chore can offer a chance to practice mindfulness. There are always dishes to wash, laundry to sort, carpets to vacuum, and a kitchen floor needing to be swept again. To integrate your mind and body while engaging in even the most routine of tasks, try this simple practice.

① Regardless of the job, begin by focusing on the entire experience of the task at hand. What's involved with this particular chore? Do you require gloves, soap, and hot water? Or do you need electricity and plug-in appliances?

② What's your body doing? Are you standing still and moving your arms and upper torso? Or are you walking around, moving from room to room?

③ What are you thinking about during this chore? Is this a chore that you've done since you were a small child? Or is this a new chore caused by some recent changes in your life, such as moving to a new house?

④ Allow yourself to find an easy pace and flow for this work. Find the little pockets of joy within the task at hand. Notice how your mindful awareness attending to the chore makes it feel more enjoyable, and you more full of life.

And, of course, when you're done, there's always the joy of having a clean house, finishing a project, or going outside to play!

feeding your body's senses

51

tides of peace

Like a good horse, your body carries you wherever you want to go, and then it needs a proper rest.

To rest deeply, use the following practice as often as you like. It will nurture every dimension of your being.

① Take a comfortable, well-supported position, in a place free from interruptions.

② Breathe mindfully for about a minute.

③ Set your intention. For example, "May this practice heal and nourish me."

④ Breathe mindfully for a few more breaths.

⑤ Gently begin to include your body sensations in your field of attention. Just notice the flow of sensations as you breathe mindfully. Be aware of all your body's contractions and expansions.

⑥ Imagine that each in-breath fills you with ease and peace. Take it all in.

⑦ Allow each out-breath to carry away your tension like an ebbing tide.

⑧ Ride the tide, receiving peace and releasing tension, for as long as you like.

52

vital nutrients

Did you know that to live and thrive, your body requires at least forty nutrients found in food? First the food gets broken down, and then the nutrients are carried into your bloodstream, where they are distributed throughout your body. Let's take this moment to visualize maximizing your body's innate ability to digest and absorb all the vitamins and minerals that it needs to stay healthy and feel good.

①   Begin with a meal placed in front of you. Take a moment to look at the colors and take in the aromas of the food.

②   Say aloud or to yourself, "With this meal, I am supporting my body's natural power to take in food and convert it to essential nutrients. With each bite, I am nourishing my mind and body with all that they need."

③   Remember to select healthy food choices and to not rush through your meals. Slow-paced meals will aid in the absorption of all the vital nutrients that sustain you throughout your life.

53

bless this food

To bless one's food is an ancient and universal human practice. Such blessings nourish our spirit, promoting feelings of gratitude, strengthening our sense of being a part of the web of life, and making us present for that which we hold sacred. Done mindfully, any blessing shines. May you find comfort and inspiration in the following blessings.

①   Before beginning your meal, pause and gaze at your food in silence.

②   Breathe mindfully for a few breaths.

③   Offer your favorite blessing.

④   If you would like to try a different blessing, consider the following:

"Earth, water, fire, wind, space,

Countless others gave their life energy that I may eat.

May I be grateful, and may their gifts benefit all living things."

⑤   If you like, reflect on the meaning of these words in your life.

all that you need

Nourishing your body means making sure you get everything you need. You cannot survive for long without the basics: water, food, warmth, and sleep. Make this the basis for your self-care checklist, and be mindful of what's missing, especially when you get swept up in your hectic day-to-day life.

① Start your checklist with the most essential ingredient: water. Have you had eight to ten glasses of pure water today? What can you do to make water more readily available? Consider keeping a water bottle near you at all times.

② What did you eat today? Do you have a tendency to get caught up in work and skip meals? Can you incorporate small breaks into your schedule so you can eat more regularly for nourishment and sustenance?

③ Do you tend to run hot or cold? By paying attention to your body's needs for warmth and coolness, you're embarking on a path toward mindfully caring for and responding to your body's needs.

④ How did you sleep last night? Do you need a nap? Consider turning in early tonight if you didn't get the rest that you needed last night.

Five good minutes in your body begins with learning how to observe and take care of your basic needs.

55

may we all be well

Nourishment takes many forms.

Kindheartedness and generosity are as crucial to well-being as the food you eat.

The practice of meditating on loving-kindness is an ancient form of meditation based on intentionally wishing yourself and others to be well.

When you next find yourself in a group or crowd of people, try it. Begin by sending kind wishes to yourself, then expand your focus to include all the others, even the strangers.

① Decide to explore deliberate kindness as a vehicle for nourishing life.

② Breathe mindfully for about a minute.

③ Set your intention. For example, "May this practice feed my heart and spirit."

④ Breathe mindfully for a few more breaths.

⑤ Begin speaking quietly in a kindly way to yourself, wishing yourself well. For example, "May I be safe. May I be happy. May I be well."

⑥ Let go of any doubts or critical thoughts, and return to your phrases.

⑦ Expand your focus. Imagine speaking the same wish to all those around you, quietly, from your heart.

⑧ "May we all be safe and happy. May we all find peace."

56

sacred eating ritual

Many cultures honor the ritual of eating as a sacred activity that connects us to nature, spirit, and the mystery of life itself. Before your next meal, try this meditation as a way to acknowledge your gratitude for the ways in which your food nourishes your health and well-being.

① You are sitting at your dining table eager to start your [meal].
Take this moment to connect with the rhythmic ebb a[nd]
of your breathing—the air being first drawn into your lungs,
filling your chest, and then its release, out past your nose.

② Consider carefully the food in front of you. What's in it?
Where did it come from? Who grew it? How did it get from
where it was grown to your home?

③ Open yourself to a place of conscious gratitude for the food
you are about to eat.

④ Say aloud or to yourself, "In this silence, I acknowledge
this food as a gift from nature. I am grateful for this food's
miraculous life-giving qualities."

⑤ Now take a moment longer to savor the aroma before you take
your first bite. Enjoy!

57

your bath awaits

Mindful attention can reveal unsuspected richness and evoke deep appreciation for almost any experience—including your bath or shower.

Let this gentle practice guide you through the landscape of mindful bathing.

① No matter how rushed or how relaxed you are feeling, pause before stepping into your bath or shower, and breathe mindfully for a few breaths.

② Let your mindful attention include your whole body and all of your senses.

③ Set your intention. For example, "May I nourish myself with kind attention and find greater happiness here and now."

④ Paying attention mindfully as you move, step carefully into the water. Open softly to the stream of sensations; feel the moisture, warmth, tingling, and pressure. Widen your focus to include all the sensations your body is experiencing.

⑤ As you choose, also include sounds, sights, aromas, and even tastes in your mindful attention.

⑥ Let go of any thoughts you are having, neither fighting nor following them.

⑦ Bathe and refresh your entire being.

58

the food-mood connection

The science of nutrition includes the significant connections between food and our minds and emotions. The food you eat can affect your emotions. The same research also shows how feelings affect food choices. How does food affect your feelings and vice versa? The next practice allows you to follow your food-mood relationship. If you want an in-depth understanding of your own food-mood connections, start a food journal to track your feelings before and after meals.

① Before preparing a meal or grabbing a quick snack, pause and take a minute to check in with your emotions. What sort of mood are you in—grumpy, impatient, serene, elated?

② Consider the foods that you select in terms of the mood you're in. How do your emotions influence your healthy versus unhealthy food choices?

③ After you make your food selection, pause and reflect on how these foods might affect how you will feel after you eat. Do you usually feel irritable and rushed, tired and lethargic, or pleasantly full and content after a meal?

④ Consider the foods that might have played a role in how you're feeling right now. How would a light meal versus a heavy one affect your emotions?

When you become more aware of the food-mood dynamic, you will empower yourself to make better food choices that will relax or energize you and enable to you think more clearly.

59

settle into peace

Have you ever noticed how the faster your thoughts are racing, the faster your body wants to move? Or the faster your body is moving, the faster your thoughts will race?

Such is the mind-body connection.

Learn to slow down mindfully and release those unconscious habits of hurrying and worrying.

① When you are feeling agitated in mind, body, or both, acknowledge that agitation and yourself compassionately.

② Set your intention. For example, "May I discover more peace and ease in myself."

③ Breathe mindfully for a few more breaths.

④ Consciously link your breath to a deliberate body movement. For example, inhale as you raise up your arms and slowly exhale as you bring them down. Or step forward, walking on the out-breath, and completely stopping on each in-breath.

⑤ Breathe and move mindfully for a minute or so. Then sit down and cease all voluntary movement.

⑥ Breathe mindfully and allow peace to fill you.

60

living foods

Holistic nutritionists assert that whole or living foods—foods direct from nature without human intervention—contain more nutritional content and value than processed foods, such as bread, pasta, crackers, or freeze-dried or canned foods. Nutritional value is the essential difference between processed or packaged foods versus fresh, unprocessed, whole foods, such as fruits, veggies, whole grains, meat, legumes, nuts, and seeds. You can make a mindful effort to bring more "live" foods and beverages into your diet in the following ways:

- Make a colorful salad that contains a wide spectrum of the rainbow, such as dark leafy greens, purple cabbage, yellow tomatoes, red onion, carrots, beans, cucumbers, apples or pears, raw walnuts or pecans, and other favorite veggies.

- Consciously cook extra food at dinnertime, so you'll have leftovers for lunch the next day, instead of eating out.

- Be aware of replenishing your body with water, fresh fruit juice, and herbal tea throughout the day, instead of soda, coffee, and alcohol.

Making more mindful—and nutritious—food choices can go a long way toward helping you feel better living in your body.

61

bite by bite

Each bite of food provides nourishment, but how many of your bites do you actually taste, or even notice?

Mindful eating simply means paying attention on purpose and nonjudgmentally to the total experience while you are eating, and as long as you continue to eat.

Eating mindfully is actually easier than you may think. And it creates the real possibility of nourishing yourself deeply, while enjoying every bite of your meal.

① Whenever you wish, before eating a meal, decide to eat mindfully.

② Set your intention. For example, "May eating mindfully nourish me in new ways."

③ Pause and look closely at your food, noticing shapes, colors, size, texture, and even the empty spaces on your plate.

④ Stop to smell your food. Sense the sharp and subtle fragrances, the familiar scents, and the new aromas. Try to focus on the direct experience of the aromas, not getting lost in the name or a story about the smell.

⑤ When biting and tasting, let yourself notice the sensations of biting, chewing, and swallowing. Pause between bites. As for tastes, notice the textures, sweetness, saltiness, tartness, sourness, and bitterness.

⑥ While chewing, notice how the textures and flavors change, how the food is ground up by your teeth, and then how it disappears when swallowed.

⑦ Throughout your meal, pause often to gently notice what you are doing. Relax and enjoy, bite by bite.

62

a meal with heart

To eat more consciously requires being more present when you eat and not taking your food for granted. Imagine if every bite of your food was more appreciated. Learning to appreciate your meals can help to remind you of your connection not only to your food, but with the source of the food, and of your connection with all living things. The following heartfelt meditation will help you to feel more connected to yourself, others, and the world around you.

① Before you begin your next meal, bring your attention to your breath. Notice when you breathe in and when you breathe out.

② Hold the intention of being grateful and appreciative of the food set before you. Say aloud or to yourself, "I am aware of the work and preparation that went into this meal. I am grateful for the soil that grew the vegetables, the farmer who picked the produce, the animals that grazed the land, and the truck that delivered the food to my market."

③ Engage your heart by infusing this meal with your loving energy.

④ May each bite conjure up deep, caring, and thoughtful feelings within you.

63

soothe your pain and fear

Because of the amazing connections between mind and body, unpleasant physical sensations such as pain can interact with a powerful emotion; for example, fear—only to create additional discomfort and suffering.

Pain and fear form a kind of feedback loop, in which each stimulates the other until they both dominate your consciousness.

Pain and fear, however, can be worked with by using mindfulness and compassion. It is worth doing that work. Even one moment of mindfulness can interrupt the distressing synergy of pain and fear, and promote peace, healing, and hope.

① When experiencing physical pain (and fear), decide to work with the situation using mindfulness and compassion.

② Set your intention. For example, "May this practice bring me peace and ease."

③ Bring your mindful attention directly to the area of your body where the painful sensations are occurring. Breathe mindfully as you focus more sharply. Let your mindful breathing flow in and out exactly where the pain is located. Let your breath penetrate and fill the area that hurts and the painful sensations alike.

④ As you breathe, imagine speaking to yourself and your body mercifully, saying something like "May I be at ease and well. May I be safe and filled with peace."

⑤ Befriending and comforting yourself, rest in kindness and mercy.

64

chew your food

If you've been in the habit of rushing through meals and wolfing down your food at lightning speed, you may be inadequately chewing, digesting, and absorbing what you eat. If you don't get the nutrients that you need every day, then you might not feel your best. You may feel overly tired or even experience brain fog after you eat too hurriedly. Take five minutes to slow down and give your body a chance to really soak up all the necessary vitamins and minerals you need to keep you healthy.

① First, avoid distractions by turning off the television, radio, or CD player, and putting away any books or magazines. Create a space for silent serenity.

② Become aware of the cycle of your breathing—inhale and exhale—balancing your breath slowly, gently, and rhythmically.

③ Imagine a calm energy circulating around the room and entering your body, then traveling from the top of your head, down through your spine, and to your arms and legs, fingers and toes.

④ Position your hands side by side, palms down, directly above your meal. Just send and receive energy to and from the food.

⑤ Let go of your thoughts about your day. Leave behind any desire to rush to eat your meal.

⑥ Now, gently take a bite of food. Chew slowly and methodically, savoring every flavor. Keep your intention focused on absorbing the most nutrients out of every mouthful.

65

the gift of silence

The busyness of living all too easily distracts us from our wholeness and from our deepest nature as human beings.

Turning your attention toward silence can help you become less distracted.

After a moment of silence, it easier to watch the return of thoughts and the sense of urgency—but not to identify with them. You may find wisdom through presence.

Reconnect with nourishing silence using this practice.

① For this practice, turn off or put away the sound-making devices on and around you. Choose not to fight or follow other sounds beyond your control.

② Breathe mindfully for about a minute.

③ Set your intention. For example, "May this practice restore ease and peace within me."

④ Continue to soften and open, breathing mindfully.

⑤ Include sounds in your awareness. Listen to tones, volume, duration—just the pure sound—letting all thoughts go, without struggling.

⑥ Find the silence in the moment before and after each sound occurs. Return to the silence when your attention moves.

⑦ Rest in that silence; rest in that peace.

66

the elements of food

In your frantic morning schedule, you might race out the door, either skipping breakfast or making do with only coffee. In your hurry, you may have lost sight of the vital relationship between your body and nature. Luckily, it's not been lost for good. Let's reconnect right now. You can use this practice while you shop for groceries, prepare food, or just before you eat.

① Begin by contemplating your connection to the land where your food grows and to the four elements that contribute to that growth: earth, water, sunlight, and air. The food on your plate is infused with these four forces of nature.

② Speak your intention aloud or to yourself: "I thank the wind for shaking the seeds to the ground. I thank the soil for providing a bed for seeds to grow. I thank the water for feeding the seeds. I thank the sun for germinating the seeds and helping them grow."

③ From the farm to your plate, both you and the land prepared this meal together.

67

intend to nourish

The most ordinary actions often have a nourishing purpose, even if their nurturance is not consciously recognized. Of course, a sip of water or a bite of food carries sustenance, but what about sitting down to relieve your tired feet, or stretching to ease a stiff muscle?

What if you paid more attention on purpose to the nourishing and encouraging power present in countless moments of daily life? What if you consciously added positive affirmations to these ordinary activities to practice intentional self-care?

Explore and play with this practice, and see how simple, yet powerful, nourishing yourself can be.

① Acknowledge the possibility of self-nourishing during any daily activity you like.

② Breathe mindfully for a few breaths and focus more steadily.

③ Add some affirming phrases to the activity as you continue doing it. For example, "Eating this food, I nourish my body." "Brushing my teeth, I am taking care of them." "Stretching gently, I comfort my body." "Learning something new, I strengthen my mind." Or, "Holding my partner, I nourish our love."

④ Keep it simple. Be present, noticing, acting, intending to nourish, caring.

68

read the label

In terms of nutritional value, although homemade meals made from scratch are the ideal, these days we can't help but rely on a few packaged foods. Who has time to soak the beans or wait for the bread to rise? Do the next best thing: Read the labels and understand the nutritional facts. Here are some mindful tips for interpreting deceptive labels in your pursuit of good health:

- *Total fat:* Not all fats are unhealthy. To stay healthy, some fat is essential. But be aware of the trans-fat numbers or the partially hydrogenated oils in the ingredients list. These oils pose a risk to human health.

- *Calories:* If you're counting calories, remember not all calories are nutritionally equal. For example, a diet soda provides fewer nutrients than a fruit yogurt smoothie.

- *Total carbohydrate:* Know the difference between refined and whole carbohydrates. Refined carbohydrates, such as those found in bread, pasta, or cookies are highly processed foods that quickly break down into simple sugars. Complex carbohydrates that break down slowly and provide sustained energy are found in fresh fruits, veggies, beans, and whole grains.

- *Sugars:* Check the ingredients for added sugars, such as high-fructose corn syrup, maltose, and sucrose, as well as artificial sweeteners.

69

this sweet moment

Joy, peace, and ease are deeper and closer than you may think.

Too often, your mind thinks that something really desirable is not here where you are, but somewhere else. When denying the goodness of the present moment, your mind takes you away from the very sweetness you seek.

Let this mindfulness practice reconnect you with the treasures and blessings in the here and now.

① The next time you are feeling happy—when you are alone in nature, with loved ones or a beloved pet—decide to experience the present moment more deeply and then move further into your happiness.

② Set your intention. For example, "May paying attention mindfully enhance my joy."

③ Steady your attention by taking a few mindful breaths, or by focusing mindfully on the flow of your bodily sensations.

④ Open your focus to include all that is happening in and around you. Gently pay attention on purpose, see the others, hear the sounds, be aware of the flowing sensations in your body.

⑤ Notice, smile, and release any thoughts you may have, without judgment or struggle.

⑥ Present in this moment, relax, and enjoy all the joy you are feeling.

70

body signals

The hectic pace of life today may keep you on the go. You might skip meals or turn to coffee (or other stimulants that unnaturally suppress your appetite). Is it sometimes hard to know when you're hungry? Do you wait to eat until your thinking has already become muddled, and you feel anxious or irritable? Appetite awareness is an important part of nourishing your mind and body to maintain top performance. Here's how to become more conscious of when you need to eat.

① What does hunger normally feel like to you? How does your body alert you that it's time to eat? Does your stomach growl or churn? Do you experience difficulty with maintaining focus and concentration?

② Consider the time frames when you normally eat. For example, do you have breakfast at 7:00 AM, lunch at 1:00 PM, and dinner at 6:30 PM? And when do you like to have snacks?

③ Allow these time frames to be reminders to check in with your body. Don't avoid or ignore your body's signals telling you that it needs food. If you're prone to forgetting to eat, you may want to set an alarm or post a note as a prompt to yourself.

avoid the temptation

Dieticians often recommend eating a few healthy snacks between meals to balance blood sugar levels and curb sugar cravings throughout the day.

Do you find it challenging to make healthy snack choices? Are you often surrounded by donuts, cookies, or boxes of chocolates in the lunchroom at work?

Here are some nutritious snack combinations that you can easily fix to take with you before you race out the door on an empty stomach, and fall prey to a world filled with "decadent" temptations:

- Fruit and nut combinations, such as pears and almonds, apples and walnuts, oranges and cashews, or bananas and pecans

- Veggies and dips, such as carrots and hummus, celery and nut butter, or cucumbers and bean dip

- Yogurt and a handful of trail mix

- Hard-boiled eggs

- Cheese and whole grain crackers

Remember to keep a variety of snack options on hand; make it easy so you can pack it and take it with you wherever you go. Keep it organic too!

72

listen and respond

When you really think about it, you are always a part of larger bodies. Air flows in and out of your body, other bodies, and the atmosphere of our planet. Energy leaves the sun, illuminates your visual field, and guides your movements. Biologically, you came into a nuclear family, with extended family relations and connections. Socially, you live and work in communities of others.

Let this next practice help you focus on the amazing interconnections of smaller and larger bodies in the universe, and the possibilities for peace and healing through presence and compassion.

① The next time you are in any group, try an experiment.

② Pause and breathe mindfully for a few breaths.

③ From a base of ease and relaxation within yourself, gently and respectfully begin to notice the others more mindfully. Look at each person, listen without wanting to change or fix anything, and stay present and open to what is happening.

④ As you observe others, include your own inner life in your focus, breathing mindfully and releasing any struggles. Continue breathing, listening, and noticing—mindfully.

⑤ Quietly ask yourself something like "What is needed now? What is the wisest response?"

⑥ Let wisdom and compassion guide your next action.

73

after-meal meditation

How often do you take the time to connect with your body after you've finished eating? Perhaps you scarf down breakfast and speed off to work, or you grab lunch at your desk while reading e-mails, or it's dinner and then a movie to preoccupy you for the rest of your evening. Try something different and follow this mindful after-meal meditation.

You've just taken your last bite. You feel full and comfortable. Savor the last few tastes on your tongue. What aromas are still emanating from the kitchen or dining area? What bodily sensations do you feel? Food can give you pleasure, warm you up, and make you smile inside and out.

74

hand to hand

All food from nature has a life force, or energy, be it a living seed, vegetable, fruit, grain, or animal. The Chinese refer to this energy in all living things as *chi*. Many people believe that the energy input from the humans who grow and handle your food also infuses the food. Become conscious of the human path of energy that touches your food in the following practice.

① Hold a piece of fruit or a vegetable in your hand, or simply hold a mental image of one that you like to eat, such as a strawberry, carrot stick, or baked potato.

② Take a moment to think about when the plant was just a seed. Imagine who it was who planted it in the soil.

③ Now contemplate the hands that went into cultivating and harvesting the plant.

④ Consider the many hands that sorted and cleaned your fruit or veggie.

⑤ Think about the hands that boxed your food and drove it to the market, followed by more hands that unloaded it and put it on display in the produce aisle.

From seedling to your plate, the fruit or veggie was touched by the hands of many people, filling it with a special vibrancy and love. This is not something you can get from a vending machine or from highly processed and packaged foods.

75

an atmosphere of calm

Creating a peaceful calm environment while you eat is the key to healthy eating and greater satisfaction with your food. Take a moment to reflect on creative ways you can enhance your dining experiences. Here are some suggestions to get you started:

- Gather the family (or friends and roommates) to dine together and keep the conversation light and agreeable.

- If alone, light a candle to remember the ones you love who are seated with you in spirit.

- Avoid unnecessary distractions, such as television or the newspaper, which might deliver distressing news.

- Savor your food, chewing slowly to fully appreciate each bite, one bite at a time, and honor the gift of nourishment the food brings to your body.

- Honor and respect your body by eating only when you're hungry and not hurried, and remember to stop eating once you've begun to feel full.

wise body

76

mindful acceptance

Your relationship with your body and how you view it can affect everything you do in life. When you're feeling well and looking good, you give little thought to where you go or whom you might run into. But if you're feeling self-conscious or preoccupied with something you don't like about your body, then you might avoid other people or situations where others might see your perceived flaws. For example, one woman admitted that when her acne flared up, she spent days isolating at home. This next exercise will teach you how to accept your body nonjudgmentally.

① Begin by observing the negative thoughts and criticisms that you have toward your body, such as "I'm fat and ugly" or "I'm too scrawny and need more muscles" or "I hate my thighs."

② Take a quiet moment to experience these random negative thoughts. Then, begin to practice nonjudgmental acceptance of yourself by saying aloud or thinking, "I'm not perfect. This is the body that I was born with and I am learning to accept myself without judgment."

③ At this time, you are simply observing any discomforting thoughts and not reacting. Notice your thoughts but resist any inclinations to agree or disagree. You are merely accepting that you have thoughts, that these thoughts come and go, and that they are always changing.

④ One mindful way of paying attention to your negative thoughts is to respond to them by acknowledging what you observe about your body, and then to practice acceptance without attaching a judgment or opinion of yourself or your body.

77

your body, your friend

W hen you think of the friends in your life, do you think of including your body?

When you think of your body, does it seem like a stranger—or an opponent?

What a difference consciously treating your body as your friend could make!

Try this next practice and see for yourself.

① Take a comfortable position. Be sure you are well supported and safe from interruption.

② Breathe mindfully for about a minute.

③ Set your intention. For example, "May this practice help me care for my body better."

④ At your own speed, and in no particular order, begin to bring mindfulness to the sensations flowing in different parts of your body.

⑤ As you settle on an area of your body, open yourself to those sensations and imagine speaking directly to them with affection, using words like "May you be at ease. May you be healthy. May you be protected."

⑥ Notice and learn from any feelings that follow.

78

dear body

In your life you've probably written countless letters to partners, friends, lovers, and family. But have you ever written a love letter to yourself? Take a few minutes to write, seal, stamp, and deliver this letter addressed to your body. Here's how to get started:

① Select nice stationery or a card.

② Imagine you are a secret admirer who wants to seduce you with every word. Get creative with your letter; it should make you blush with delight.

③ Begin with "Dearest Beautiful Body" and list at least three things you love about your body. For example, a man might write "This is a love letter to remind you that you have a very sexy butt, gorgeous strong hands, and the kind of hair that screams out to be touched." A woman might write, "This is a love letter to remind you that you've got the sexiest curvy hips, soft supple skin, and a smile that brightens people's day."

④ Seal your letter in a self-addressed envelope, and send it off.

79

rest easy, dear one

When your body hurts or is injured, one common reaction to the pain and vulnerability is to become angry or rejecting.

Yet, when your loved ones or friends are hurt, kindness and compassion fill your heart.

Explore the healing potential of meeting your own body's pain with compassion instead of anger by using this practice.

① Noticing pain or injury in your body, pause and take a comfortable position, protected from interruption.

② Breathe mindfully for about a minute.

③ Set your intention. For example, "May this practice bring me peace and healing."

④ Gently focus mindfully on your body area in distress.

⑤ Soften and open to the sensations there, allowing and releasing them. Allow and release any thoughts or stories in your mind. Notice and release any anger you feel.

⑥ Imagine speaking with mercy to your body. Say, "Rest easy, dear one. May you be safe and well."

⑦ Let kindness and compassion support you.

80

follow your heart

You may live most of your life as if your mind and body were running a race, frantically moving from place to place with people to see and tasks to accomplish. Can you slow down? Can you imagine living your life from your heart? Let's turn our attention from our racing minds to our hearts. When you live your life from your heart, you allow your emotional compass to point toward a path of compassion and kindness. Let's try it now.

Your heart meditation starts by listening to and connecting with your feelings. All emotions are important, even the unpleasant and painful ones. Try to simply acknowledge them and not to judge whatever feelings emerge. You may feel unsettled or restless. You may notice a pocket of sadness or regret that's been suppressed for a while. Your emotions are what make you human, and they give you the opportunity to open your heart to the limitless capacity for compassion and tenderness you have for yourself. Allow your heart to guide your life.

81

attend, befriend, and surrender

Psychotherapist and author Miriam Greenspan writes poetically about the dark emotions that live in the body, and she describes how to befriend and surrender to this kind of suffering in order to heal through gratitude. The following meditation will guide you through the process of transforming something difficult into something valuable.

① Focus your attention on your emotions and where they live in your body. For example, your frustration with a coworker might reside in your neck and shoulders, or your grief after a messy divorce might dwell in your chest. Listen and attend to your body's emotional language.

② Befriending requires you to stay with a difficult emotion and not run away. Essentially, you act like a compassionate and loving friend to yourself, while you move further into your emotionally tender place.

③ Take this moment to breathe several times into the place where your negative feelings live.

④ The final stage, which is to surrender to your suffering, takes courage. It involves radical acceptance of your emotions. You mindfully accept and endure the natural flow of feelings without suppressing, trivializing, or minimizing them, which will lead you to the gift of understanding, greater wisdom, and healing.

You will come to learn that only through awareness can fear lead to serenity, and that despair can open you to harmony.

82

not so different

You know how fear feels in your body. And anger. And pain. And hunger.

Perhaps you've recognized these conditions in others as well, by their expression or appearance.

This next practice uses mindfulness and compassion to reveal your deep connections and intersections with other people more consciously.

① Choose a place safe from interruption, and take a comfortable position.

② Breathe mindfully for about a minute.

③ Set your intention. For example, "May this practice help me to feel less alone."

④ Recall someone you know who is suffering. He or she may be afraid, in pain, angry, or homeless and hungry.

⑤ Breathe mindfully, keeping that person's image in your heart.

⑥ Imagine speaking gently to that person. Say something like "May you be free from your suffering and pain." Keep repeating your wish silently, like a chant.

⑦ Shift your focus to yourself and any pain you feel. Wish yourself freedom from pain and suffering. Say something like "May I be at peace and at ease."

⑧ Allow mercy for yourself and the other person to comfort and console you.

83

you are not alone

Do you ever find yourself fixated on a part of your body that you hate, or obsessed with certain foods? Do you spend hours, days, maybe years, self-absorbed in a perceived physical inadequacy, yo-yoing between the latest fad diets? The next practice will help to steer you away from the self-destructive cycle of hating your body.

You are not alone with your obsessive feelings and self-hatred of your body. Millions of men and women, young and old, are plagued with the same emotional challenges and the same critical inner voice. Here's a meditation that will help you feel less alone.

Now, imagine that you are sitting in a room filled with some of these people. When you look around, you see friends, coworkers, and strangers—all struggling, just like you, to reach an impossible ideal of perfection. You can see the desperation in their eyes. You begin to feel the stirrings of a true sense of connectedness with everyone in the room. Your well of compassion and empathy for yourself and others lies here. The longer you sit, the more your feelings of understanding and tenderness will spill over to encompass both you and the others. You are all in this together.

84

at peace with change

How often and how easily we meet bodily illness or pain with denial or aversion.

Getting angry with whatever is uncomfortable can be painful. But our discomfort may remind us of how vulnerable we are to change; so it may be easier to get angry than to face change.

Creating a different relationship with the difficult is possible and can be healing.

Use this practice to develop your own compassionate response to the truth of change and the mortality that resides within everyone.

① The next time you face illness or pain in your body, stop and take a comfortable position.

② Breathe mindfully for about a minute and set your intention. For example, "May I gain wisdom to meet and soothe my fears."

③ Focus mindfully on the area of most distress in your body. Let the sensations there flow through your awareness, as you breathe mindfully with them.

④ Look closer. Acknowledge your changing sensations, thoughts, and emotions connected with this area of pain or illness. Have mercy on them and yourself as you breathe mindfully.

⑤ Let your attention to the changing elements become steady. Rest in the steadiness. Notice how every sensation, thought, and feeling is changing.

⑥ Can you let go of resisting the change?

85

loving-kindness for one and all

Drawn from an ancient tradition of Buddhist meditation, compassion training has been shown to activate areas of the brain that increase a sense of well-being and decrease stress. Let's try this compassion practice now.

① Begin by becoming aware of any physical sensations in your body, particularly around your heart. Hold your intention to diminish suffering and to send loving-kindness—or great friendliness—to yourself and to others.

② Start with yourself. Say aloud or to yourself, "May I be healthy, happy, and at peace." Repeat this phrase three times slowly. Breathe into the areas of your body that yearn for sympathetic attention.

③ Now think of another person. Think of someone you know who is suffering. It can be someone you know personally or someone you don't know. Say aloud or to yourself, "May you be healthy, happy, and at peace." Repeat this phrase three times. On your exhale, breathe out empathy for the other person, who, like you, yearns to be loved and acknowledged.

④ Now try to imagine all living beings. Say aloud or to yourself, "May all beings be healthy, happy, and at peace." Repeat this phrase three times. On your exhale, breathe out loving-kindness for all beings, great and small.

86

a prayer for healing

Prayer is a form of meditation—it is a quiet time for setting a heartfelt intention, and for holding a mindful awareness of the present moment. Use this next practice to send healing intentions to your body. You can easily make it a part of your everyday routine.

① Find a quiet, calm place to sit or kneel comfortably. Feel free to close your eyes. Tune in to the pattern of your breathing, in and out, rise and fall.

② Pay attention to the area of your body that causes you the most pain or suffering. Maybe it's your heart? Perhaps it's your head? Could it be your stomach?

③ Visualize that specific part of your body as if it were being held very gently and safely in your loving arms.

④ As you hold this part of your body in your loving embrace, say aloud or to yourself, "This prayer holds the power of healing intention. May I experience relief and serenity throughout my body."

87

kindness to moving bodies

Whether you are traveling alone, on foot, in a car, or accompanying other moving bodies as a part of a group on a train, a bus, or a plane, or you are simply waiting in a terminal, a train station, or an airport—your body, when traveling, remains a part of the body of the world.

This practice invites you to explore the power of kindness as your body moves with other bodies through intense fields of hurry, worry, and distractedness.

① The next time you are traveling, in the midst of the hurry and intensities of the situation, consciously decide to shift your focus and to experiment with the qualities of kindness and compassion.

② Set your intention. For example, "May this practice benefit me and others."

③ Steady your attention by taking a few mindful breaths.

④ Look around mindfully. Just notice what is happening around you without judging or trying to fix or change it.

⑤ Respectfully and gently notice other people. Are they excited, happy, angry, sad, worried, or afraid? Continue mindful breathing as you look more closely.

⑥ Imagine speaking to one or more of those you see. Wish that person peace and safety, happiness and ease. Say something like "May you be safe and happy." Repeat your well-wishing silently and as often as you like.

⑦ What do you discover?

88

safe haven

You can probably draw up a long list of what you dislike about your body. You hate your prominent nose, or giant mole, or noticeable scar. Maybe you've spent countless hours thinking about getting plastic surgery. What if someone were to tell you that some day someone will fall in love with that special spot on you, and all that makes you unique and beautiful is stored right there? Let's take a moment to go on a retreat from being mercilessly self-critical about your looks and shortcomings.

Visualize yourself boarding a plane headed to a tropical paradise. You arrive safely and are transported to a perfect, peaceful setting. You are feeling relaxed in your body and stress free. You didn't pack a care in the world. It's just you and the sand, the fresh air, and the sound of seagulls. No one else is around, so let it all hang out. Take your jacket off and stay a while. Don't worry about what you imagine other people are thinking. Just unwind, take in the breathtaking surroundings, and let those inner voices get swept away by the breeze. Let your negative criticisms be washed away with the ocean waves. You are truly a gorgeous creature, inside and out.

89

dear body, thank you

Regarding your body, it's easy to focus on what you don't like, but how often do you shift your attention to what works well and is good?

Appreciating your body for how well it actually does work can radically transform your experience of being in your body.

Try this practice of mindfully thanking your body and see what you discover.

① Take a comfortable, well-supported position in a place safe from interruption.

② Breathe mindfully for about a minute.

③ Set your intention. For example, "May this practice deepen my gratitude for my body."

④ Remember a specific body function that serves you well—one that works just fine. Perhaps it's your vision or hearing, your arms or legs, or your ability to think.

⑤ Imagine speaking kindly to your body and thanking it for this gift.

⑥ Breathe mindfully for a few breaths and say, "Thank you, dear body; thank you for my life."

90

the journey of forgiveness

If you've spent a lifetime hating your body, it may not be easy to come to terms with your past behaviors and forgive yourself. It's not simple, but with patience and practice you can learn to love and transform those behaviors. Let's try it now.

① Identify specifically what it is that you want to change and say aloud or to yourself, "I intend to do something to change this about myself." It could be overeating or starving yourself, or eating unhealthy foods.

②   Make a mental or written list of the feelings and thoughts that surface when you think about your body or food issues, such as anger, depression, anxiety, or loneliness.

③   Now envision replacing your old behavior with a new response. Imagine that you're about to eat an entire bag of potato chips to fill the emptiness you feel. Envision stopping yourself and saying, "I don't have to let my emotions make my choices. Today I'm doing it differently."

④   Visualize yourself picking up an apple, slicing it, eating it, and experiencing a delicious satisfaction for the first time.

⑤   Take this moment to open your heart to the infinite capacity to love and forgive all that is good or bad, fair or unfair, all that just is. Say aloud or to yourself, "Change takes time. I am moving with patience and tolerance. I am committed to letting go of the painful thoughts I impose on myself. I am learning to forgive."

91

choose kindness

Although your attention may move between past, present, and future, you are actually living in the present moment. Life is happening right now.

One powerful question to ask is this: "In this moment, how am I treating life?"

Check it out. Stop and pay mindful attention to your inner reactions and to the tone of your thoughts.

Then, try to keep it simple. Decide to choose kindness.

① Wherever you are, whenever you choose, breathe mindfully for a few breaths and return to this moment.

② Set your intention. For example, "May I recover my open heart and generous spirit."

③ Notice and allow any critical or doubting thoughts or judgments, without struggling with them. Breathe mindfully, allowing them to be.

④ Consciously shift your attention from criticism to kindness. Begin with yourself and your own body. "May I be happy and at peace." Think of another person. "May you be happy and at peace."

⑤ Keep it simple. May all be well.

92

earth intimacy

The Omaha Indians perform a ceremony for a newborn infant that celebrates the intimacy between the universe and humans. The following exercise, adapted from this tribe, acknowledges the interconnection and dependency of humans not only on the planet, but on the larger community needed to sustain life. Take this moment to recognize your covenant of mind, body, and soul with the earth and all her splendid gifts.

① It's best to be outdoors for this meditation. Find a tree to stand under or lean against, or sit on the grass. Get as close to nature as you can.

② Say aloud or silently, "Dearest Sun, Moon, Planets, Stars, and beyond. Thank you for your gifts that light my path. We are one in our sharing."

③ Say aloud or silently, "Dearest Sky, Clouds, Rain, and Snow. Thank you for your gifts that feed the earth. We are one in our sharing."

④ Say aloud or silently, "Dearest Sacred Earth, Humans, Plants, Animals, and all beings on the planet. Thank you for your gifts of nourishment. We are one in our sharing."

You are affirming your life-giving agreement with Mother Earth and all living things above and below.

93

mercy for your sick body

It happens so often. You meet an illness in your body with anger. Amazing, isn't it?

You wouldn't think of being angry at a friend for being sick.

This practice invites you to cultivate mindfulness and compassion in the service of peace and healing for your body, heart, and mind whenever you are ill.

① Take a comfortable position in a place where you won't be disturbed.

② Breathe mindfully for about a minute.

③ Set your intention. For example, "May this practice aid my healing."

④ Bring merciful attention to the area of your body that is ill. Breathe mindfully as you focus there, imagining the breath moving gently in and out through that area.

⑤ As you breathe, imagine speaking to your body gently, as if to a friend. Say something like "May you be safe and well."

⑥ If it feels right, offer forgiveness as well. "For any hurt or difficulty you cause me, I offer you forgiveness."

⑦ Include all parts of yourself that are suffering. Hold all with mercy and caring.

94

your gratitude list

You know it's a good idea to make a list of what you're grateful for, but you just don't get around to actually doing it. So take the next five minutes and do it now.

① Grab a pen and paper.

② Start with your body and record what you're most thankful for. You may list good health, good energy, flexibility, being able-bodied, strong hands and back, good hugger, great kisser, and so on.

③ Next, focus on your mind and what you're most thankful for. You may list alert, witty, good sense of humor, friendly, approachable, attentive, conscientious, and so on.

④ Last, make a list of what you're most grateful for in your life. You may list partner, friends, family, children, siblings, walking, camping, sports, making love, and so on.

Keep your written list on your fridge at home or tape it to your computer monitor at work as a reminder of what truly matters in your life.

95

nourishing the body and soul

If you read the book or saw the movie *Like Water for Chocolate*, then you might be familiar with how your emotions can affect the food that you're preparing in both positive and negative ways. For example, if you slap together a boring sandwich when you're feeling depressed, it's possible that you've infused your sad feelings into your food. Whether you believe this concept or not, there's something to be said for imbuing food with good energy to feed both your body and spirit.

236

① Before you hurriedly prepare a meal, pay attention to what you're feeling. What emotions are skimming the surface of your life right now? Discontent? Annoyance? Confusion?

② Before handling your food physically, shake out your arms, legs, and torso. Imagine that you can hear your heavier, darker emotions jingling like loose change in your pocket. Picture the coins spilling out and disappearing.

③ Be mindful of just one thing that you're feeling appreciative about in your life. Hold that thought front and center in your mind while you begin to prepare your food.

④ Be conscious of imparting loving-kindness into your food to feed your body and soul.

96

in praise of your body

Oh wondrous body! Oh mysterious flesh, organs, and skin! Let me count the ways that I love thee. You may not be perfect, but you are perfectly extraordinary, perfectly magical, so rare and unique in every way. Celebrate your body by listing what's working, what gives you life, and what you appreciate. Sing your song of praise for your body aloud or to yourself:

Oh glorious body, you are magnificent! I give praise to every bone, piece of cartilage, and sinew. I give praise to every organ—liver, pancreas, spleen, heart, brain, glands, lungs, intestines, and more. I give praise to every blood cell, proton, and drop of water within me. I give praise to my eyes, ears, mouth, and nose. I give praise to my arms, legs, torso, neck, and head. I give praise to every fingernail, toenail, layer of skin, freckle, beauty mark, and hair.

Every inch of you is a remarkable gift of life!

97

see the miracle

Albert Einstein is said to have observed that you can live your life in two ways: as though nothing is a miracle or as though everything is a miracle.

Having a body that works can be viewed this way, too.

Use this practice to help reveal the miraculous happenings in your very own body.

① Give yourself some time and space in a place where you won't be disturbed.

② Breathe mindfully for a few breaths.

③ Set your intention. For example, "May this practice awaken wonder and joy in me."

④ Bring mindful attention to one hand. Move your fingers, extending, gripping, touching each to your thumb, stretching, and flexing.

⑤ Notice with increasing sensitivity the elements of your experience: stillness, intention to move, movement, and all of your sensations.

⑥ Reflect on the miracle of having a body that can move and does so willfully, linked to the thoughts in your mind. Recognize that such movement is not guaranteed forever; let gratitude come.

98

water reverence

The human body cannot survive more than a week without water. From water we were created, and from water we are born. In many ancient religions and cultures, water plays an important role in everyday life. Create your own water ceremony to acknowledge water's powerful vitality and life-giving powers. Here are some suggestions:

- Wash up before you eat. Cleanse your face, neck, hands, and arms. You are purifying your mind, body, and soul in a symbolic gesture before your meal.

- Give appreciation for water. When you water your plants, fill your water bottle to drink, turn on the faucet to cook, clean, or make tea, take a moment to appreciate this miraculous, clear liquid of life.

- Pour yourself a glass of water and take a few sips. Feel the water moisten your lips, mouth, teeth, and tongue. Notice the sweetness. It's refreshing and satisfying. Imagine the water renewing and replenishing every cell of your body. Give thanks.

99

the end of resentment

Feelings of resentment are your interior reactions—physical and emotional—to certain interactions with others who make up some of the larger bodies of your life.

Learning to practice forgiveness—the end of resentment—can deeply benefit your body, mind, and spirit, and benefit the others in those larger bodies.

① The next time you feel annoyed or upset with someone, decide to experiment with forgiveness instead of criticism.

② Take a comfortable position in a safe place, and breathe mindfully for about a minute.

③ Set your intention. For example, "May this practice bring me wisdom and peace."

④ Breathe mindfully for a few more breaths, steadying your attention and relaxing.

⑤ Shift your attention to the upsetting person. Looking deeply, see the pain and confusion within that person.

⑥ Now, imagine speaking gently to that person. Say something like "For any harm you have caused me, intentional or unintentional, I offer forgiveness. I wish you peace."

⑦ Let forgiveness bring you understanding and direction.

100

dear body, I am sorry

When you are out of touch with your body because of hurried and worried thinking or distracted attention, you can easily contribute to physical harm or illness.

All the while, your body tries faithfully to do what you ask of it. Use this next practice to soothe and heal body and mind, and to nurture your well-being.

① Take a comfortable, well-supported position where you will not be disturbed.

② Breathe mindfully for about a minute.

③ Set your intention. For example, "May this practice bring me well-being."

④ Relax and breathe mindfully for a few more breaths.

⑤ Widen your focus and mindfully include the flow of all bodily sensations. Noticing, sensing, receiving, allowing.

⑥ More in touch with your body, imagine speaking gently: "For any harm I have brought you, intentional or unintentional, please forgive me." Speak to any part or your whole body, as you choose.

⑦ Meet any reactions—in body or mind—with mercy and kindness.

Jeffrey Brantley, MD, is a consulting associate in the Duke University Department of Psychiatry and the founder and director of the Mindfulness-Based Stress Reduction Program at Duke's Center for Integrative Medicine. He is author of *Calming Your Anxious Mind* and coauthor of *Five Good Minutes, Five Good Minutes in the Evening, Five Good Minutes at Work, Five Good Minutes with the One You Love, Daily Meditations for Calming Your Anxious Mind*, and *The Dialectical Behavior Therapy Skills Workbook*.

Wendy Millstine, NC, is a freelance writer and certified holistic nutrition consultant who specializes in diet and stress reduction. She is coauthor of *Five Good Minutes, Five Good Minutes in the Evening, Five Good Minutes with the One You Love, Five Good Minutes at Work*, and *Daily Meditations for Calming Your Anxious Mind*.

UQ NO HT YIK QK Q10